THE HIDDEN MEANING AND POWER OF THE LORD'S PRAYER

based on the Syriac Aramaic

SHAHAN SHAMMAS

WORTHWHILE PUBLICATIONS

Copyright © 2025 SHAHAN SHAMMAS

All rights reserved
No part of this book may be reproduced or transmitted in any form or by any means, electronic or mechanical, including photocopying, recording, or by an information storage and retrieval system–except by a reviewer who may quote brief passages in a review to be printed in a magazine or newspaper– without permission in writing from the publisher. For information, please contact the author at shahanshammas@gmail.com

Although the author and publisher have made every effort to ensure the accuracy and completeness of information contained in this book, we assume no responsibility for errors, inaccuracies, omissions, or any inconsistencies herein. Any slights on people, places, or organizations are unintentional.

ISBN-13: 9780966202861
Printed in the United States of America

To my wife, Barbara, and my daughters Olivia and Emily and their husbands Ben and Antony. To my grandchildren Dylan and Chloe. To the brave souls everywhere unafraid to question their beliefs, open their eyes to see, clear their ears to hear and examine their hearts to discern the truth.

CONTENTS

Title Page
Copyright
Dedication
Part I   1
Introduction   2
What is Prayer?   17

Part II   29
Our Father   30
Who Art in Heaven   50
Hallowed Be Thy Name   60
Thy kingdom Come   78
Thy Will be done on Earth, as it is in Heaven   93
Give Us This Day Our Daily Bread   110
Forgive Us Our Debts, As We Forgive Our Debtors   124
Lead us not into Temptation   139
Deliver Us from Evil Part I   151
Deliver Us from Evil Part II   163
For Thine is the Kingdom, the Power and the Glory,   171

Forever and Ever Amen	183
Part III	189
How to Pray for Results	190
Part IV	215
How to Re-enter the Kingdom of Heaven	216
Conclusion	233
Appendix	235
How one book altered the course of my life	236
Acknowledgement	251
About The Author	253

PART I

Introduction

What is Prayer?

INTRODUCTION

How often have you heard or recited the Lord's Prayer? What does it mean to you?

Why did Christ teach us this particular prayer? Are there hidden gems buried within it that we need to discover?

Is this a generic prayer that anyone can use anytime they feel like it? Or, is it an incredibly powerful prayer that once we know how to utter it with awareness and intent, it can transmute us forever?

Our Father who art in heaven
Who is this Father we are praying to? And where exactly is heaven? Is it up in the sky somewhere? Can it be a feeling in our hearts and minds?

Hallowed be Thy Name
Do we know God's name so that we may hallow it? How can we find out what this name is? If God has a name, isn't that a limitation, a confinement?

Thy kingdom come
What exactly is this kingdom and why are we asking for it to come? Is the Kingdom of God the same as the Kingdom

of Heaven? Do we know exactly what we are asking for?

Thy will be done on earth as it is in heaven
Are there two wills, one on earth and the other in heaven? What is God's will? Is there any other will than that of God's and can this other will be expressed instead of God's will?

Give us this day our daily bread
Does this mean we do not have to earn our livelihood? Do we just ask for it instead? Besides, why are we limiting ourselves to bread only? What about some meat and vegetables as well? Even better, how about a sumptuous meal and a lavish dessert while we are at it?

And lead us not into temptation
Who leads us into temptation? Is it God or the Devil? If it is the Devil, why are we asking God not to lead us into temptation? Isn't that what the Devil does?

But deliver us from evil
What exactly is evil? And if God does deliver us from evil, does it mean that we do not face evil anymore?

I was born in Aleppo, Syria. As a young boy, I went to the Syriac Orthodox elementary school where I studied Syriac which is a form of Aramaic and went to the Syriac Orthodox Church daily. Along with the rest of the liturgy, I recited the Lord's Prayer in Syriac Aramaic.

At the age of 15, I went to Lebanon where I joined the Syriac Orthodox Monastery in Zahle, Lebanon to study Syriac Aramaic and prepared to be a monk.

After 2 years, I left the monastery and went to Southern Lebanon to complete my High School education. Then I went to the American University of Beirut where I graduated with a degree in Biology. I immigrated to the United States, joined the US Army for three years, got married, worked for the Government for 30 years, retired, taught adult education for 10 years, authored several books, and conducted workshops and seminars on all aspects of spirituality for over 30 years. One of the favorites topics I lectured on was: **The Hidden Meaning and Power of the Lord's Prayer based on its Syriac Aramaic.** I have spent many years studying Christ and His teachings and what I discovered hidden in the Lord's Prayer is remarkable and amazing.

First, a word about my interpretation

It is a well-known fact that there are numerous versions of the Bible, a multitude of Christian sects and denominations each with its own interpretations of the Bible and what the teachings of Christ mean.

I have studied spirituality for over 40 years and continue to do so. My insights into the hidden meaning and power of the Lord's Prayer are based on my understanding of spirituality. I strongly believe that <u>**Christ was a spiritual teacher**</u>. He was not sectarian trying to establish a religion. Religion is predicated on having followers, and the more the better. Religion demands obedience and acceptance of Orthodox interpretations of the scriptures based on faith and that particular religion's understanding and emphasis.

Christ's intention was to empower us as individual

Children of the Father, not as sheep and followers. He wanted us to know that whatever He did, we could do also:

> *Verily, verily, I say unto you, He that believeth on me, the works that I do shall he do also; and greater [works] than these shall he do; because I go unto the Father. John 14:12*

Christ wanted us to know that the Kingdom of God was within us:

> *Neither shall they say, Lo here! or, lo there! for, behold, the kingdom of God is within you. Luke 17:21*

If the kingdom of God is within us, so is God.

This kingdom was clearly not physical. It was spiritual:

> *Jesus answered, "My kingdom is not of this world. If my kingdom were of this world, my servants would have been fighting, that I might not be delivered over to the Jews. But my kingdom is not from the world." John 18:36*

Christ had to couch the essence of His teachings in parables to avoid persecution and premature death. To paraphrase Christ, the people He was dealing with **"had eyes, but couldn't see, had ears, but couldn't hear. They had hearts hard like stone"**. Fortunately, He was able to complete His mission prior to being crucified for what He stood for. He did this by teaching the people through parables. The only ones He taught openly were His disciples and only when they met privately and in secret:

> *Then the disciples came and said to him, "Why do*

> *you speak to them in parables?" And he answered them, "To you it has been given to know the secrets of the kingdom of heaven, but to them it has not been given. For to the one who has, more will be given, and he will have an abundance, but from the one who has not, even what he has will be taken away. This is why I speak to them in parables, because seeing they do not see, and hearing they do not hear, nor do they understand. Matt 13:10-13*

I view the Lord's Prayer as another parable. Buried deep within it are some incredible insights as to what Christ had in mind when He taught us this prayer. To "see" the hidden meaning and power of the Lord's Prayer requires that we be fearless, approach it with an open mind and heart and be willing to accept new insights. We know an insight is genuine and true if it sets us free, especially from limiting beliefs. For a complete revelation of what the secret teachings of Christ within the parables are, please refer to my book: **_The Secret Teachings of Christ, based on the parables_**.

There are two paths we can choose from; the wide, paved highway used by most and the road less travelled used by the few. Most choose the wide and easy path to follow. This is the path of religion. It requires little effort and involves almost no thinking. We just have to believe, accept and follow. Those who choose the second path, the narrow and more demanding, are few. This is the path of spirituality. It involves effort, requires reasoning, the courage to question, to doubt, to stand out, and at times, to be shunned.

Generally, religion teaches that we are born in sin and require redemption. We are sheep in need of a shepherd.

The belief is also that once we die, we are judged. If found to be "good", we go to heaven, otherwise, we go to hell.

Spirituality emphasizes that we are Children of God, but have forgotten this truth and are living like the Prodigal Son. What we need is not redemption, but rather knowledge and spiritual truth that sets us free of superstition, fear and ignorance. The foundation of spirituality is not belief, but rather experiential knowledge. Spirituality espouses that our fate in in our own hands. We determine our future by the choices we make and the actions we take. We do not require anyone else to redeem us. We must do it ourselves. We must redeem ourselves from our own ignorance, selfishness and immaturity.

There is a great deal of evil in the world stemming from ignorance, fear and superstition. The best way to confront evil is to be an agent of light. The more understanding we have the brighter our light shines. This book is intended to be a torch that dispels some of the darkness. The hope is that by discovering the spiritual teachings of Christ hidden in The Lord's Prayer and in His parables, our vision will clear so we see and hear better and, in the process, we become more compassionate, loving and caring. Each of us is like a lit candle. Together, we are a power to reckon with. We can illuminate our surroundings.

The views expressed in this book are a complete departure from what is expected. Some are even radical. Please do not reject them offhand. They require time to incubate. Evaluate them and ask for guidance. The Voice Within will guide us to know what is truthful and what is falsehood. The litmus test is that truth will always set us free:

> *and you will know the truth, and the truth will set you free." John 8:32*

To unearth the truth hidden in the Lord's Prayer, we must have an open mind and be willing to hear new, controversial and challenging views. We must be fearless. We have three guides to help along the way: mind, heart and the Voice Within. Let them be your guide.

Before we begin explaining why Christ taught us this particular prayer, its spiritual significance and the transformative power hidden within it, a brief history of Aramaic and the setting in which this prayer was given is required.

Aramaic

> **Aramaic is a** Semitic language closely related to Hebrew. Originally the language of the Aramaeans, it was used in Mesopotamia and Syria before 1000 BC and later became the lingua franca of the Middle East. Hence, when Jesus said anything attributed to him, he said it in Aramaic—the language common to the entire population of Palestine at the time. Ancient inscriptions in Aramaic have been found from Egypt to China. Aramaic began to decline in favor of the Arabic language at the time of the Arab conquest in the 7th century AD. Aramaic survives today in scattered communities in Syria, Lebanon, Turkey, Iraq, and Iran. *(Adapted from Wikipedia)*

The Syriac language

> Syriac, a Semitic language was the Aramaic dialect used at Edessa and in Western Mesopotamia. It was similar to, but not identical with, the Aramaic dialect used in Palestine during the time of Jesus and his apostles. *(The Interpreter's Dictionary of the Bible)*

The language Jesus spoke was Palestinian Aramaic. What I studied and am basing my interpretation of the Lord's Prayer on, is Syriac Aramaic—"similar to, but not identical to the one used by Jesus".

Aramaic is a rich language where a word not only can have multiple meanings, but where a slight variation can change the meaning of that word or sentence. As an example, the word *"halo"* means dust. If we read it as *"helo"* it means vinegar. If we read it as *"holo"* it means sand. If we read it as *"hale"* it means sweet, pleasant to the taste. It's the same word, yet the meaning can vary tremendously with a slight variation in ***accent***.

Words used in a sentence can also have multiple meanings. They can have a symbolic significance which is different from its obvious meaning. For example, the word *"garden"* can have a meaning that is beyond the obvious. In the Songs of Solomon, the term *"garden"* was the conventional symbol for the body of the bride.

It is the nature of Semitic languages including Aramaic, Arabic and Hebrew to allow for various interpretations. One word or even a letter can have several meanings. That is why there are numerous translations with varying interpretations of the same sacred passage in the Bible. Those who study the Kabbala, for example, come to understand that within the Hebrew alphabet lies hidden the key to profound spiritual laws. That each letter has phonetic, numerical, and mystical values. So it is with Aramaic. Letters, words and sentences in Aramaic can have multiple meanings and hold within them the key to profound spiritual laws and truths.

The setting

Christ taught the Lord's prayer as part of the Sermon on the Mount. He told his listeners: *And when you pray; first, you go to your house, close the door, and pray to your father in private. And your father who sees you in secret will reward you openly.* When He says go to your house, close the door, (or enter your closet), the literal meaning is obvious. There is, however, a symbolic or a spiritual meaning as well. House, can mean *privacy,* a sanctum or a clear *mind.* We enter our *"house"* and we shut out the outer world. If we do not understand the culture of the people and the context in which these words are used, we could miss the hidden significance of what was really meant. Most translators give the obvious and literal meaning of a word and that can be shortsighted.

Why did Christ teach us this specific prayer?

One of the best ways to preserve metaphysical concepts is through stories, allegories, parables, rituals, symbols and cryptic writings. This is also what Christ did. When He wanted to explain something to the people, he told stories, usually in the form of parables. Only His disciples were fortunate enough, or ready enough, to hear the message unambiguously.

Christ did not teach us this prayer so that we parrot the words. He did it because these words hold a spiritual significance. Unless we dig into them, their meaning will elude us. Christ was clear that He did not teach the people anything openly, only through parables:

> *All these things spake Jesus in parables unto the multitudes; and without a parable spake he nothing unto them. Matt 13:34*

Does this mean that the Lord's Prayer itself is a parable?

The Sermon on the Mount is the heart and soul of Christianity. Since the Lord's Prayer was taught as part of the Sermon on the Mount, it must have a special significance. This prayer is the only specific instruction Christ gave, not only on how to pray, but what exact words to use. In Matthew 6 beginning verse 5, He says:

> *And whenever you pray, do not be like the hypocrites; for they love to stand and pray in the synagogues and at the street corners, so that they may be seen by others. Truly I tell you, they have received their reward. But whenever you pray, go into your room and shut the door and pray to your Father who is in secret; and your Father who sees in secret will reward you.*
>
> *When you are praying, do not heap up empty phrases as the Gentiles do; for they think that they will be heard because of their many words. Do not be like them, for your Father knows what you need before you ask him.*

And the King James Version states:

After this manner therefore pray ye:

> *Our Father which art in heaven, Hallowed be thy name. Thy kingdom come. Thy will be done in earth, as it is in heaven. Give us this day our daily bread. And forgive us our debts, as we forgive our debtors. And lead us not into temptation, but deliver us from evil: For thine is the kingdom, and the power, and the glory, forever. Amen.*

The specific instructions of where and how to pray, raise a few questions we need to consider, for example:

1. How can we pray for something, if everything is determined by natural law? Are we asking God to put aside these natural laws in order to favor us and grant our request?

2. If God is Omniscient and knows what we need before we ask Him, why do we need to pray at all? If we are God's children, then we already have everything we need. What are we praying for?

3. Finally, if we are to go into our room and shut the door and pray to our Father who is in secret, why do we have so much group prayer and in public places such as churches, synagogues, mosques and even schools?

Obviously, there must be some deeper and hidden meaning to what Christ said. We need to take a closer look.

To fully understand the spiritual significance of what we read in the Bible it helps to know, not only Aramaic,

Hebrew and Greek, but more importantly, we need to understand allegory, metaphor and symbols. It also helps to know history, geography, archaeology, culture and the traditions of the area, how people lived, what they believed and practiced, and how they transmitted knowledge. This last one has a special significance.

When I was young and living in Syria, telling stories was the way the locals transmitted knowledge. My father was a storyteller. I remember many nights the neighbors would gather where we lived and my dad would start telling stories. Listening to these stories as a young boy, I believed in their literal meaning. The stories were real and true for me because I didn't know any better. I would hear my dad tell the stories and the way he made up the stories was so realistic that I thought they were factual.

Storytelling was how knowledge was transmitted in the ancient world and many were versed in storytelling. Storytellers, however, were not as sophisticated as those who invented and made up stories. Most stories were for entertainment and socialization, A few, however, were specifically crafted to contain "hidden and secret" knowledge. The parables of Christ and the Lord's Prayer fall into this category. Hence, what the common person understood by a story, is not necessarily what the sages intended by those stories.

Stories convey the belief and understanding of the people. Through stories, people interpreted the mysteries that surrounded them. If people wanted to understand creation, they made up a story on how creation might have taken place. They solved their mysteries by creating stories that explained them.

As a child, when I heard the stories my dad told, I did not see any deeper or hidden meaning in them. For as long as I remained a child, I could not see anything else in the stories. It was only after I studied spirituality that I had a better understanding of the hidden and deeper meaning and power of some of those stories.

The Lord's Prayer is a sacred teaching. As such, it can be interpreted on various levels. We can consider it as a simple and beautiful prayer and overlook its significance. That would a shame. By taking a closer look, we discover a treasure trove of gems buried within it. The spiritual teachers of old bequeathed us gifts of immense value in the form of storied and parables. These gifts must be unwrapped to reveal their deeper and hidden meaning. That is what we are going to do with the Lord's Prayer.

There are 4 levels of interpreting sacred writings (Hieroglyphics) such as the Lord's Prayer:

1. The first is the simple interpretation. We merely accept the writings as they are. The Gnostics call this level of interpretation "**hylic**" or the surface and material level. At this level, we accept the writings at face value and view them as literal truth and historic fact. Many do just that. That is their prerogative and it is not wrong, but that's just scratching the surface of interpreting sacred writings. We need to dig deeper to get to the "*seeds of truth*" hidden beneath. Since the literal and mundane meanings are evident and obvious; they are called **exoteric**;

2. The second level of interpreting sacred writings

is the acknowledgement that there is a deeper meaning to them, and that they are symbolic, figurative, and allegorical. The Gnostics call this level of interpretation "**psychic**" or the mental interpretation. At this level, we realize that these stories are allegories. In other words, they stand for something else that is a deeper truth and this truth is not self-evident. It must be excavated. This is what the Lord's Prayer and the parables of Christ are like;

3. The third level of interpreting sacred writings is the spiritual. The Gnostics call this level "**pneumatic**". At this level we realize that there is a hidden, deeper, and spiritual meaning to the writings. We come to understand that these writings contain profound **spiritual** laws and truths. The spiritual meaning of a passage is often hidden and secret; hence, it is called **esoteric**;

4. The final level of interpreting sacred writings is the *personal* level. Here we apply the teachings to our personal lives. We cease to analyze. We simply know based on our personal experience. We cognize what the writings mean. They have a special meaning to us personally. We do not need any proof. We simply know what they mean. We have a **Gnosis**.

The Lord's Prayer in Syriac Aramaic

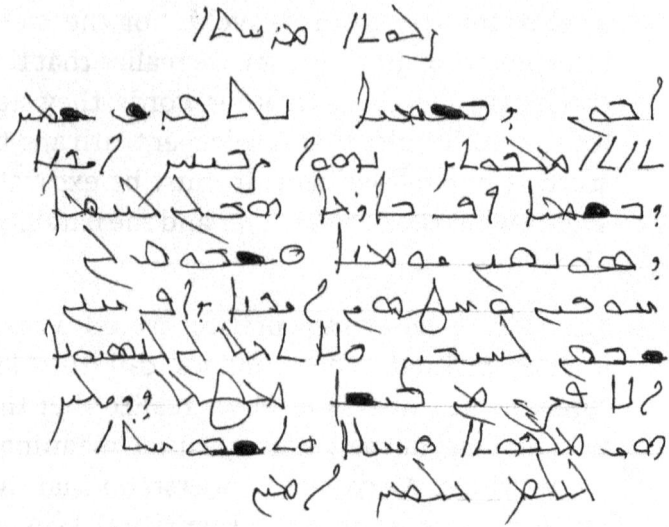

The transliteration of the Syriac Aramaic
prayer reads as follows:

Aboon d bashmayo
Netqadash shmokh
Teeteh malkuthokh
Nehwe sebyonokh aykano d bashmayo oph b aroh
Hablan lahmo d soonquonan yaomono
Wa shbooq lan haobayan wahtohayn
Aykano d oph hnayn shbowqan el hayobayn
Olo tehlan el nesyuno
Elo phason men bisho
Metool dilokhi malkutho o haylo o teshbuhto
L olam olmin ameen

WHAT IS PRAYER?

The idea seemed to be that if you prayed extremely hard—especially if a lot of people prayed at once—maybe God would change things. The trouble was, what if your enemy was praying, too? Which prayer would God listen to? —Jeanne DuPrau

There are times when we feel a strong inner urge to pray. This happens when we find ourselves with no other alternative. In the movie "Arn", his mother prayed passionately for the life of her son Arn after he fell from a high location and became unconscious. I, too, have prayed with all of my heart for the recovery of my daughter who was very sick and having difficulty breathing. Even Christ prayed at His darkest hour:

And he went a little further, and fell on his face, and prayed, saying, O my Father, if it be possible, let this cup pass from me: nevertheless not as I will, but as thou [wilt]. Matt 26:39

We must have an innate urge to appeal to a "higher

authority" when all else fails. We pray because we believe that an intervention is possible.

Prayer is defined as, *"a reverent petition made to God, a god, or another object of worship."* Another definition is, *"prayer is an act of communion with God, or another object of worship, such as in devotion, confession, praise, or thanksgiving."* A third definition is, "p*rayer is an awareness of, and a response to the presence of God in everyday life."* I like this last definition the best.

Each religion or sect has its own method of prayer and perhaps a different object of worship as well. While many pray to God, others pray to saints, angels or to transcendent beings. Regardless of who we pray to or how we pray, the mere act of praying indicates that we believe that we are not alone. We acknowledge that there is "someone" more powerful and listening. We also believe that we are either connected to the object of our prayers or that there is a way our prayers are heard and can be answered. If we did not believe this, we would not pray.

Since we use words to pray whether silently or vocally, we must also believe that there is someone or an intelligence that can understand our language and that this intelligence can make out what our intentions are and respond accordingly.

If prayer is communion with divinity, then we either find this divinity within us and commune with it, or we must establish a link to it through prayer if it is outside of us as most do. Either way, we must connect to this divinity if we want our prayers to be heard.

Most link to divinity by way of ritual. This ritual could be as simple as going to a place of worship such as a church, a mosque, a synagogue, a holy site or a sanctuary of some sort. Any preparation prior to prayer such as ritualistic washing and purification or even fasting is an aid to help us prepare and establish contact with the divine.

Since communication is a two-way street, for our prayer to be effective, there must not be only talking, but more importantly, listening as well. This is why in Syriac Aramaic the word for prayer is: "*sloto*" from the root word "*slo*" which literally means "to trap" or "to set a trap" implying the setting of oneself as a trap to catch the thoughts of God. This is usually accomplished through meditation and introversion. To master prayer, we need to master the art of listening. This listening must be attentive, exclusive and anticipatory.

Types of Prayer

People pray silently or aloud, using made up words or reciting from memory. People pray fervently or nonchalantly. There are several types of prayers:

1. Informal prayer is when we talk to God informally asking for help or giving thanks. We may say something like: "God please let my child make it home safely". Or, "God please help me recover from this illness. I promise to take better care of myself". This is prayer of intercession which is of two types: we pray for what we want to happen and we also pray for what we do not want to happen. For example,

if it has not rained for a long time and we have a draught, we pray for rain. On the other hand, if it has been raining too much, we pray for the rain to stop and for sunshine to appear;

2. Ritualistic prayer is when we go to a house of worship and recite our prayers in a prescribed manner. We repeat a predetermined sequence of words. Often, this type of prayer is a statement of a creed, of what people believe in. Prayers of creed are **ritual expressions that reinforce our convictions of what we believe, accept, and know to be true.** In other words, this form of prayer is a review of our belief system. It is a statement of our worldview;

3. Prayers of confession involve both acts of commission and omission. We pray for the things that we did that we should not have done and we pray for the things that we did not do that we should have done. For example, if we made a mistake, we pray for forgiveness or if we should have acted but did not, we pray for courage and wisdom to act the next time the situation arises;

4. Prayers of supplication is an appeal for something specific such as the birth of a child. There are several examples of this in the Bible where barren women engage in this type of prayer requesting a child to be born and promising in return to dedicate the child to the service of God. Examples are Samson and John the Baptist;

5. Prayers of adoration are general expressions of praise, love and devotion;

6. Prayers of petition are when we pray for another asking God to intervene on their behalf;

7. Meditation is a form of prayer where we sit silently and introvert. There are two phases to meditation: An active phase where we contemplate Love, Beauty and Joy and a passive phase where we empty ourselves of all thoughts and become receptive to the promptings of the Voice Within.

Spiritual prayer

Spiritual prayer is communion with the God within and submission to its will. Even though many believe that when they pray, they are praying to a God somewhere out there, since God is everywhere, the closest God is within us. Hence, when we pray, we are accessing our deepest and most sublime aspect of our self, the Higher Self, which is an aspect of God residing within us. This Self is always connected to God and is part of the divine. If we commune with our Higher Self and allow it to function through us, then we are living a life of prayer.

Why do we pray?

People pray for many reasons: out of habit, because of a need, while feeling helpless, as a result of fear, to worship, to adore or simply to commune with God or a transcendent being. People pray on all occasions: weddings, funerals, baptisms, communions, before eating, before going to war, before sleeping and after waking up.

We are inundated with prayers; in schools, houses of worship, TV and radio. Even terrorists pray before they carry out their intended acts. Here is a prayer printed in the Washington Post on Friday September 28, 2001 and excerpted from a five-page handwritten document that the FBI found in Mohamed Atta's luggage. Translated from Arabic:

> *God, I trust in you, I lay myself in your hands. I ask with the light of your faith that has lit the whole world and lightened all darkness on this earth, to guide me until you approve of me. And once you do, that's my ultimate goal.*

To pray to God to ask for things is folly. It is as if we are accusing God of withholding from us. Didn't Christ say:

> *When you are praying, do not heap up empty phrases as the Gentiles do; for they think that they will be heard because of their many words. Do not be like them, for your Father knows what you need before you ask him. Matt 6:7-8*

We should not pray to ask for things because whatever we are asking for is already given to us. What we can do instead is to pray for enlightenment so that we know what **we, ourselves,** need to do to bring about that which we seek. In other words, instead of asking for things, we can ask for the wisdom to know what actions we can take to bring about what we want. We need to take charge of our lives and realize that we have what it takes to act on our own. All we need is the wisdom to know what our next step is and the courage to do our best.

General vs. personalized prayer

Some prefer to recite what they already know, while others like to make their own prayers. What is important is not the words we use, but the spirit in which we use these words. Where are the words coming from? The lips or the heart? Are we parroting or are we aware of every word we are uttering?

There are times when it is preferable to use our own words when we pray and there are other times when the pre-written words are so beautiful and moving that we use them instead. We are stating our convictions when we pray regardless of what words we use. Our words and thoughts are an outpouring of what we believe in.

An example of prayer as a statement of belief is the Nicene Creed which is recited by many Christians.

The Nicene Creed

> *We believe in one God, the Father All-sovereign, maker of heaven and earth, and of all things visible and invisible; And in one Lord Jesus Christ, and the only-begotten Son of God, Begotten of the Father before all the ages, Light of Light, true God of true God, begotten not made, of one substance with the Father, through whom all things were made; who for us men and for our salvation came down from the heavens, and was made flesh of the Holy Spirit and the Virgin Mary, and became man, and was crucified for us under Pontius Pilate, and suffered and was buried, and rose again on the third day according to the Scriptures, and ascended into the heavens, and sits on the right hand of the Father,*

and comes again with glory to judge living and dead, of whose kingdom there shall be no end:

And in the Holy Spirit, the Lord and the Life-giver, that proceeds from the Father, who with the Father and Son is worshipped together and glorified together, who spoke through the prophets: In one holy catholic and apostolic church: We acknowledge one baptism unto remission of sins. We look for a resurrection of the dead, and the life of the age to come.

Personally composed prayers, stemming from the heart, are powerful and effective. They are often simple, relevant and emotional. Pre-written prayers, on the other hand, are general and conventional. Reciting them often lacks sincerity, intensity and conviction. One of the popular pre-written prayers people use when lonely, fearful, and requiring comfort, is Psalm 23. This psalm starts with: **"The Lord is my shepherd and I shall not want."** Unless we truly believe that we are sheep requiring shepherding, we should avoid this prayer. If, on the other hand, we are addressing our Higher Self as our shepherd, then by all means we can use this prayer. Whatever we do, we must do it with awareness and conviction, not mindless parroting. Words are powerful especially when coupled with emotions. They impact our bodies. Words, repeated over time sink deep into our subconscious and become habits. Habits govern our lives. We should only use words that empower and ennoble and that lead to habits we want to have.

There are 3 pre-written prayers that are, not only beautiful, pure and sincere, they are also empowering, ennobling and transformative.

The **first** is a hymn of adoration composed by Akhenaton, a pharaoh of Egypt around 1350 BC. This hymn which is really a prayer is a devotional to the god Aton, the supreme god symbolized by the Sun and the outpouring of its rays.

Here are a few selected lines from this beautiful and moving ancient prayer:
(*from:* **The Life and Times of Akhnaton**, *pharaoh of Egypt, by Arther Weigall*)

> Thy dawning is beautiful in the horizon of heaven,
> O living Aton, Beginning of life!
> When thou risest in the eastern horizon of heaven,
> Thou fillest every land with Thy beauty;
> For Thou art beautiful, great, glittering, high over the earth; Thy rays, they encompass the lands, even all Thou hast made.
>
> Thou art Ra, and Thou hast carried them all away captive; Thou bindest them by Thy love.
>
> Though Thou art afar, Thy rays are on earth;
> Though Thou art on high, Thy footprints are the day.
>
> When the chicken crieth in the egg-shell,
> Thou givest him breath therein, to preserve him alive; When Thou hast perfected him
> That he may pierce the egg,

He cometh forth from the egg,
To chirp with all his might;
He runneth about upon his two feet,
When he hath come forth therefrom.

How manifold are all Thy works!
They are hidden from before us,
O Thou sole God, whose powers no other possesseth.
Thou didst create the earth according to Thy desire,
While Thou wast alone:
Men, all cattle large and small,
All that are upon the earth,
That go about upon their feet;
All that are on high,
That fly with their wings.

The countries of Syria and Nubia
The land of Egypt;
Thou settest every man in his place
Thou suppliest their necessities.
Every one has his possessions,
And his days are reckoned.
Their tongues are divers in speech,
Their forms likewise and their skins,
For Thou, divider, hast divided the peoples.

Thou art in my heart;
There is no other that knoweth thee,
Save Thy son Akhnaton.
Thou hast made him wise in thy designs and in Thy might.

The world is in Thy hand,
Even as Thou hast made them.
When Thou hast risen they live;

When Thou settest they die.
For Thou art duration, beyond mere limbs;
By Thee man liveth,
And their eyes look upon Thy beauty
Until Thou settest.
All labour is laid aside
When Thou settest in the west.
When Thou risest they are made to grow.., .
Since Thou didst establish the earth,
Thou hast raised them up for Thy son,
Who came forth from Thy limbs,
The King, living in truth, . . .
Akhnaton, whose life is long;
[And for] the great royal wife, his beloved,
Mistress of the Two Lands, . . . Nefertiti,
Living and flourishing for ever and ever."

We could almost add "Amen" to this poem because it truly is a prayer.

The **second** pre-written prayer that I love is the Prayer of Saint Francis of Assisi:

Lord, make me an instrument of Your peace.
Where there is hatred, let me sow love;
Where there is injury, pardon;
Where there is doubt, faith;
Where there is despair, hope;
Where there is darkness, light;
And where there is sadness, joy.

O Divine Master, Grant that I may not so much seek
To be consoled as to console;
To be understood as to understand;
To be loved as to love;

For it is in giving that we receive;
It is in pardoning that we are pardoned;
And it is in dying that we are born to eternal life.

And the **third** pre-written prayer that I love is the Lord's Prayer, the topic of this book.

If we need a prayer to recite when we need comforting, let it be empowering as well. The Lord's Prayer fits the bill. It is full of insights that can transform our lives. The Lord's Prayer is easy to remember because hundreds of millions of people already know and use it. Christians who go to church recite it from memory.

With this in mind, let us delve into the deeper meaning and power of the Lord's Prayer based on its Syriac Aramaic.

Here is the English version of The Lord's Prayer: (the Kings James version)

> *Our father who art in heaven hallowed by thy name, thy kingdom come, thy will be done, on earth as it is in heaven. Give us this day our daily bread and forgive us our trespasses as we forgive those who trespass against us. And lead us not into temptation but deliver us from evil for Thyne is the kingdom and the power and the glory forever, and ever. Amen.*

PART II

Our Father

Who art in heaven

Hallowed be thy name

Thy kingdom come

Thy will be done in earth, as it is in heaven

Give us this day our daily bread

And forgive us our debts, as we forgive our debtors

And lead us not into temptation

but deliver us from evil

For thine is the kingdom, and the power, and the glory, forever

Amen

OUR FATHER

You must remember, family is often born of blood, but it doesn't depend on blood. Nor is it exclusive of friendship. Family members can be your best friends, you know. And best friends, whether or not they are related to you, can be your family. —Trenton Lee Stewart

The very first word in the Lord's prayer is: "our."

What exactly do we mean when we say "our"? Do we mean our family, tribe, community, city, state or country? Do we mean only those who believe like we do? Or do we truly mean anyone and everyone without exception?

This is a serious question that we must reflect on. If we mean everyone, then this is all-inclusive. It implies we are all children of this Father. There are no exceptions. No one is excluded. Perhaps this is what Christ meant when He taught us to use this prayer, for He never excluded anyone from His love and compassion.

This word uttered with awareness and conviction automatically does away with privilege, selectivity and the concept of "The Chosen." There are no favored and no disregarded people in Christianity. All are welcome; all are accepted; all are equally loved and valued.

What about the people we do not like? What about evil people? Are they included as well? Yes, they are because we are all a family. Normally, in a family there are adult parents and children of various ages and levels of maturity. So is humanity. It is a gigantic family with adults and others each at a different stage of evolution, understanding and maturity. We cannot judge people because each is different. We ourselves have gone through the cycles of growth and maturation. We were children once. We grew up and gradually became mature adults at our current level of understanding. We all go through stages. Differences among individuals are natural and should be welcomed and appreciated. We cannot expect a child in elementary school to behave like one in college. We cannot learn calculus unless we first master basic math.

If we accept that the purpose of life is to grow and to mature physically, mentally, emotionally and spiritually, then each of us has life lessons that we are hoping to learn and master. In the theater of life each assumes a different role at a different stage based on what needs to be learned. There are no classes of people. There are no better or worse individuals. There are only people at different stages facing challenges and opportunities to master life-lessons. We are each students learning from others, and at the same time, are teachers helping others learn.

Our Father

In Syriac Aramaic, "Our Father "is one word *"aboon."*

Starting our prayer by saying, "Our Father", we are invoking the presence of someone familiar. We are calling forth and we are forcing our attention to realize that the one we are talking with is our **Father**, not a stranger. This is as if we are knocking on a door to get the attention of someone. We want our Father's attention. We are saying, "Hi Dad, here I am and I want to establish contact with you." If prayer is a communion with divinity, then the divinity we are communing with is our Father. This is an intimate communion. Calling God Father, is a unique concept intended to, not only highlight intimacy and confer familiarity, but at the same time, void the need for intermediaries. Our Father is someone with whom we have an open-door policy if we have a good relationship with Him.

The Father is our highest aspect that we can contact and appeal to. He is a part of our makeup. The Father resides within us as our Higher Self. This Father is someone we can relate to. He is not far away, somewhere out there. He is as close as our breath. He is approachable. Our Father is our doorway to God, whom we can never approach or comprehend directly.

It is significant to note that we are not saying: *My* Father — "*abee*", Instead, what we are saying: "Our Father"— "*aboon.*" By using the word "*our*", we are emphasizing that this Father is not just my father, your father, her father or his father, but rather, "*our*" father collectively. In other words, my father is everyone's father. There is one and only one Father who is the Father of All. This is intentional and highly significant for in many places Christ says that we are all members of one body.

All of us together form one family and no one is excluded

from this family. This family includes believers, heretics, Jews, gentiles, the good, the bad, the prostitutes, the nobles, the tax collectors, the criminals, the saints and everybody else. Everyone is included and is a member of this one family. This is similar to the parable of the rich man who throws a feast and everyone is invited. What is more important than the invitation is who accepts the invitation and becomes a member of this family. While the invitation is for everyone, acceptance is voluntary. It requires intentional action. It is up to us to accept the invitation and attend the feast. In other words, even though everyone is a member of the family, unless we know it and act accordingly, it does not do us any good. We remain outside the circle of the family.

By uttering, "**Aboon, Our Father**", the fact of our interconnectedness and interdependence becomes obvious. Since we all have the same FATHER, we are all related to one another. Just as the human body is composed of various cells, tissues, organs and systems, so is humanity. Being a member of a body implies that even though we have different roles and functions to play, we are equally valued and appreciated.

Obviously, we know that the Father we are calling upon is not our earthly father. Hence, we are instantly aware that we have two fathers—an earthly father and a heavenly one, a physical father and a spiritual one. This establishes the fact of our duality. We have an earthly father and are of earth and we have a heavenly father and thus are of heaven as well. We are of earth as a physical body and we are of heaven as soul, mind and consciousness. While we are linked to our earthly father genetically, emotionally, and materially, we are linked to our heavenly Father spiritually. We are stamped with His blueprint, image and essence.

There is a tremendous difference between the two fathers. While our earthly father can be a disciplinarian, stern and favoring one child over another, our Heavenly Father never does any of that. He is non-judgmental and His patience with us knows no bounds. He allows us to learn from our mistakes, wake up to our reality and find our way home, even if it takes forever.

Calling God, Father, is how Christ wanted us to think of God. This is how He referred to God, as His Father.

> So everyone who acknowledges me before men, I also will acknowledge before my Father who is in heaven, but whoever denies me before men, I also will deny before my Father who is in heaven. Matt 10:32-33

Who is this Father?

Everyone has an opinion as to who God the Father is. For some, God is a person. For others, God is a spiritual entity. Some consider God to be an overall pervading intelligence. Others say that God is love. Some believe that God can be vengeful, vindictive, judgmental and punishing. Some believe that God is aloof and unconcerned with our affairs. Others contend that God abhors evil and loves good. For me, God is the embodiment of **Love, Beauty** and *Joy*.

But what did **Christ** have in mind when he asked us to address our prayers to our Father? Christ wanted to simplify our understanding of God by instructing us to view God as a Father— "Ab." So, whenever He addressed

God, He referred to Him as "Abi", or my Father.

To know what kind of father Christ had in mind, we need to refer to one of Christ's parables —The Parable of the Prodigal Son. This parable elucidates the qualities of the Father Christ had in mind.

> *Then Jesus said, "There was a man who had two sons. The younger of them said to his father, 'Father, give me the share of the property that will belong to me.' So he divided his property between them. A few days later the younger son gathered all he had and traveled to a distant country, and there he squandered his property in dissolute living. When he had spent everything, a severe famine took place throughout that country, and he began to be in need. So he went and hired himself out to one of the citizens of that country, who sent him to his fields to feed the pigs. He would gladly have filled himself with the pods that the pigs were eating; and no one gave him anything. But when he came to himself he said, 'How many of my father's hired hands have bread enough and to spare, but here I am dying of hunger! I will get up and go to my father, and I will say to him, "Father, I have sinned against heaven and before you; I am no longer worthy to be called your son; treat me like one of your hired hands." ' So he set off and went to his father. But while he was still far off, his father saw him and was filled with compassion; he ran and put his arms around him and kissed him. Then the son said to him, 'Father, I have sinned against heaven and before you; I am no longer worthy to be*

called your son.' But the father said to his slaves, 'Quickly, bring out a robe—the best one—and put it on him; put a ring on his finger and sandals on his feet. And get the fatted calf and kill it, and let us eat and celebrate; for this son of mine was dead and is alive again; he was lost and is found!' And they began to celebrate.

"Now his elder son was in the field; and when he came and approached the house, he heard music and dancing. He called one of the slaves and asked what was going on. He replied, 'Your brother has come, and your father has killed the fatted calf, because he has got him back safe and sound.' Then he became angry and refused to go in. His father came out and began to plead with him. But he answered his father, 'Listen! For all these years I have been working like a slave for you, and I have never disobeyed your command; yet you have never given me even a young goat so that I might celebrate with my friends. But when this son of yours came back, who has devoured your property with prostitutes, you killed the fatted calf for him!' Then the father said to him, 'Son, you are always with me, and all that is mine is yours. But we had to celebrate and rejoice, because this brother of yours was dead and has come to life; he was lost and has been found.'"
Luke 15:11-32

Even though it appears that the emphasis of the parable is on the Prodigal Son, it is on all three characters: the Prodigal Son, his brother, and the father. By the way, prodigal means *"rash or wasteful extravagance."*

Christ grew up in the Middle East where the Father is someone who is the authority figure. His word is the law and he is often autocratic. He can be a dictator, very harsh and stern. He can judge, reprimand and reward. He expects respect and obedience. He can be generous or abusive. There is no opposing or second guessing the father in the ancient Middle East. His decisions are final.

The Father referred to in the Lord's Prayer has everything. He is abundantly wealthy, has two children who are both with him. The younger one asks the father for his inheritance. He wants to leave, go out into the world and have his own experiences. His father did not respond by saying: "Hey you idiot, listen to me and do as I say. You are young and do not understand the intricacies of the world. Stay with me where you are safe and secure and where your food, shelter and comfort are provided for you." Instead, the father said: "Son if you want your inheritance, here it is. I respect your decision. Go in peace."

And why was that? This is because this father is wise indeed. He not only believes in freedom of choice and treats his children as adults, but also knows that there is no learning, growing and maturing unless his children leave home and are on their own. There is no substitute for personal experience and He will not deny his son this opportunity. He gave his son his inheritance without question. "You want it, here it is. It is yours to do with as you please."

It behooves us to keep in mind that the son was not asking for money to go buy liquor, get drunk or to purchase drugs. He was asking for his portion of the inheritance so he can go out and experience the world. This is his right, his choice and his prerogative.

The son takes his inheritance and goes out into the world. He squanders his inheritance and pretty soon he doesn't have anything left. He has no money to eat. He goes to a farm and asks the farmer for a job and the farmer says that the only job he has for him is to take care of the pigs. So, this Prodigal Son lives with the pigs and he eats whatever the pigs eat, perhaps mustard seeds. After some time, this son gets tired of this lifestyle. He looks at himself and remembers his source, where he came from. He says to himself: "What am I doing here? I have a father who is wealthy. With my dad, I had everything. Here I have nothing. This is not where I belong. Let me go back to my father's house." Having reached the nadir of his misery, he gets up and starts his journey back home.

Word reaches the father that his son is on his way home. And what does the father do? This father does not confront his son as soon as he returns home and reprimand him, telling him: "Why are you back? It was your decision to leave in the first place. You already took your inheritance. Now go away there is nothing left for you here." No, that is not what the father does. The moment he hears that his son was on his way home, he goes out to meet and greet him. As soon as he can, he hugs and kisses him, and takes his robe and places it on his son. He takes his ring and jewelry and adorns his son with them. He cries with joy and accompanies his son home. He orders his servants to slaughter the fatted calf and prepare a feast. He proclaims that his son who was lost is now found and is back at home where he belongs.

What this father did is very significant. He did not judge or reprimand his son. He did not tell his son that he sinned, that he made a mistake and that he was going to be punished. He did none of that. He did the exact opposite. He acted, not in a typical way, but the way our heavenly Father would.

This father had an older son and this son was furious. He said to his father: "Hey dad, what is going on here? I have been with you all these years and you never slaughtered the fatted calf for me. You never took your robe and put it on me and gave me your jewelry. How come the son who went away and squandered your wealth is getting this treatment while I who stayed with you have never received such treatment?"

To this, the father answered, "Son, don't you know that all I have is yours? You don't need to wait for me to slaughter a fatted calf for you. It is yours. If you feel like it, give the word and have the fatted calf slaughtered. Have your own party anytime you like. You are my son and all that I have is yours. Don't you know that what is mine is also yours?"

This is the father we should have in mind when we say: "aboon", our father. This father never judges. He is loving, caring, giving and eager to receive us. He is the total opposite of a typical Middle Eastern father. This Father is *not* Jehovah, the god of the Old Testament.

Where is the mother?

What about the mother? If there is a father, there must be a mother as well. Where is she? The father in the parable had two sons, but he is not the one who bears the children. It is the mother who gives birth to children. By giving birth, she transforms the "husband" into a father.

In the parable of the Prodigal Son, there is a father but no wife or mother. We know that if there is a father, there must also be a mother, but where is she? The clue once more is in the parable of the Prodigal Son.

The qualities of the Father in the parable of the Prodigal Son are feminine qualities. They are the qualities of a mother and not of a typical Middle Eastern man. Loving, caring, giving, nurturing, forgiving, not judging, being tender hearted and embracing are *feminine* qualities. Hence, the father represents both the male and the female aspects and is the father and the mother at the same time. He is the Father by being called **the Father** and he is the mother by the qualities he exhibits and exemplifies. We know this because that is how we know somebody—by their actions and the qualities they express.

> *Thus, you will know them by their fruits.*
> *Matthew 7:20*

The fruit of this father shows us that he was both the mother and the father at the same time. Or, he was the mother disguised. The God we address as Father is meant to be androgynous who is both father and mother, male and female.

Keeping in mind that Christ lived in the Middle East and that the stories we are reading take place in the Middle East, we must know something about the culture of the area.

The Middle East is a Patriarchy. While the males are prominent and upfront, the females are hidden and out of sight. Yet they exist and are relevant. Even though it seems that the females are missing, in reality they are everywhere. Even though we cannot see them, they are implied. This is because everyone knows that we can never have a child without a female. No creation can take place without the female. If males exist, they do so because females gave birth to them.

The Bible, both the Old and the New Testaments represent Middle Eastern culture. In this culture, the prevailing habit is to de-emphasize the female characters whenever and wherever they could.

This is obvious from the story of the Prodigal son where the mother is left out and also from the fact that Jesus had several siblings, not only brothers, but also sisters. These sisters are rarely mentioned in the Bible. Here are some passages to demonstrate that.

Regarding the sisters of Jesus

> *Is not this the carpenter's son? Is not his mother called Mary? And are not his brothers James and Joseph and Simon and Judas? And are not all his sisters with us? Where then did this man get all this?" Matthew 13:55-56*

Notice that they mention the names of the brothers but not the sisters.

> *While he was still speaking to the crowds, his mother and his brothers were standing outside, wanting to speak to him. Someone told him, "Look, your mother and your brothers are standing outside, wanting to speak to you." But to the one who had told him this, Jesus replied,*

> *"Who is my mother, and who are my brothers?" And pointing to his disciples, he said, "Here are my mother and my brothers! For whoever does the will of my Father in heaven is my brother and sister and mother." Matthew 12:46-50*

No mention of any sisters here.

Here is a third example:

> *Then his mother and his brothers came to him, but they could not reach him because of the crowd. And he was told, "Your mother and your brothers are standing outside, wanting to see you." But he said to them, "My mother and my brothers are those who hear the word of God and do it." Luke 8:19,*

The same event is in Mark 3, but here the sisters are mentioned:

> *Then his mother and his brothers came; and standing outside, they sent to him and called him. A crowd was sitting around him; and they said to him, "Your mother and your brothers and sisters are outside, asking for you." And he replied, "Who are my mother and my brothers?" And looking at those who sat around him, he said, "Here are my mother and my brothers! Whoever does the will of God is my brother and sister and mother." Mark 3:31-35*

Even though Jesus had sisters, in three of the four instances above that describes the same event, the sisters are left out. Only one of them mentions his sisters. What we read in the Bible is the male writer's version of the story and not necessarily the whole story.

Another example of this is that of Adam, Eve, and their children. Adam knew Eve and they had Cain first and then Abel. After Cain killed Abel, we are told that Cain knew his wife and she conceived and bore Enoch.

Who was Cain's wife and where did she come from if the only people in the world were Adam, Eve, and Cain? Thus, the female must exist.

By saying "Aboon", Our Father, we are not only invoking the presence of our father, but at the same time, we are remembering the qualities of this Father. He is loving, forgiving, kind, compassionate, willing to give us whatever we ask and is ready to receive us when we come back to Him. This Father is really a mother at heart and is a combination of both. He is both the father and the mother, male and female. He is our parent and our source.

As a final example as to why I believe that the Father we are invoking is both Father and Mother at the same time, we need to refer to the story of creation.
When God created Adam, he created him in his own image.

> *Then God said, "Let us make Adam in our image, according to our likeness; and let them have dominion over the fish of the sea, and over the birds of the air, and over the cattle, and over all the wild animals of the earth and over every creeping thing that creeps upon the earth." So God created Adam in his image, in the image of God he created them male and female he created them.*
> Gen 1:26-27

If God created Adam in His Image and Adam was both male and female, so must God be. Hence, God our Father is also God our Mother.

Members of a special family

What did Christ mean when He wanted us to think of each other as members of the same family? Picture Jesus sitting somewhere and He is teaching. There is a crowd around him. Soon his physical family comes to see him and when the people see Jesus's family, they say to Him: "Hey Jesus your mother, your brothers and your sisters are here to see you." He looks at them and says:

"Who are my brothers, and my sisters, and who is my mother"? And he points at the crowd around him and says: "you are it; you are my family because you and I have the same spiritual Father or Parent. We share the same spiritual values."

This concept of belonging to a spiritual family is powerful indeed. If we can wholly identify with this teaching, then we can immediately solve almost all of our problems. We can form family ties and bonds of love with anyone with whom we share the same ideals and spiritual values.

I always feel at home among family. I have been in several cities where I was among people with whom I shared ideals and spiritual values. Having just met, we can spend long hours together in close fellowship. We enjoy sharing meals together and spending many hours in discussion. This is because we know and feel that we are truly brothers and sisters. We are members of one and the same spiritual family.

This is exactly why in some mystical or spiritual organizations members call each other brother and sister or Frater and Soror. This is also why the priest or a clergyman is called Father or Padre. This is to remind us that we are all children of the one Father, Parent, God our source. If we can adopt and practice this one powerful concept, our lives and the world would change forever for the better.

Personal example

As an example of the power of relating to others, feeling at home, and knowing that we belong to one family, in a recent trip to Toronto, Canada to conduct a weekend retreat, I met several incredibly lovely individuals. There was one in particular that I was so comfortable with that I felt she could easily be my sister. When I returned home, I decided to adopt her as a sister. I wrote the following poem to commemorate the occasion.

I Am a Miner

When I was a little boy people asked me:
Little boy, what do you want to be when you grow up?
Without hesitation I said: A great soccer player.
A few years later, my answer changed.
I want to be an inventive scientist.
I want to investigate, discover, and innovate.
A few years later, my answer changed.
I want to be a philosopher for I love to know.
I yearn to understand life and solve its mysteries.
A few years later, my answer changed.

I want to be a spiritual person and delve into the unknown. And through firsthand experience, unravel its secrets.

A few years later, my answer changed.

Now that I am grown up, I finally know what I want to be.

I want to be a miner.

I want to mine the world for its precious gems.

Some seek wealth by acquiring money. Others pursue it by increasing their holdings and possessions. While many quest to enrich themselves through enterprise, I decided to get wealthy by becoming a miner.

You see the world's greatest wealth has eluded the majority. It is not precious stones that make one wealthy. Earth's truest wealth is it's living creatures, especially the people.

Obviously, not everyone is of the precious gem quality. The ones who are, are scattered here, there, and everywhere.

To discover them, one must have the keen senses of a miner.

I am a miner and I am out to find gem quality people.

I mine people by establishing deep and abiding relationships.

I am wealthy to the extent that I cultivate relationships with gem quality people.

The deeper and more lasting the relationship,

The more precious the gem becomes and the wealthier I get.

Obviously, it is not easy to uncover precious stones. So, when I do find one, my heart rejoices and my spirit soars.

I am a miner and a wealthy one at that.

My wealth is the loving relationship that I have with my true and lasting gems, my spiritual family.

As my family grows, so do I, and so does my wealth.

I am a miner of precious people and I am out to mine.

I am prospecting for precious gems and wondering if you are one.

If you are and I mine you, then our roles change. We are no longer the miner and the mined. We become family.

I am glad that I am finally grown up and know what I am.

I am a miner, and a good one at that.

I choose my site, I dig my ground, and lo and behold , there you are!

In summary

Just by uttering the first two words of the Lord's Prayer, (one word in Syriac Aramaic) we are immediately empowered.

Aboon—Our Father. Instantly we know who we are—you and I are each a child of God, the Father. By knowing who we are, we are 50% on our way. To attain complete power and the privileges of being the child of God, we must know not only who we are, but also who everyone else is and we must act accordingly. We must display the full aura and confidence of our position as children of the Almighty.

This requires practice and after many lifetimes of trials and tribulations, one fine day we will wake up and say: "I know who I am. I know who you are. We are family and we are royalty." "Namaste." I recognize the God in you as the same God who is in me.

To get us to this Gnosis, to knowing who we are, to acting and living accordingly, we require this world and all that it has to offer in terms of challenges, trials and tribulations. These experiences help us wake up.

Before we leave this concept of belonging to a family and the practice of living life as if we are all members of one gigantic spiritual family, I would like to share a quote from my book, **A Passion for Living, a path to meaning and joy.**

This quote is on page 272:

> We can learn to love others if we view them as family and friends. It is common practice to consider only blood relatives as family and non-family members that we like and do things with as friends. This is a narrow and parochial view. A more expansive outlook would be to consider as family anyone and everyone with whom we establish close, loving and abiding relationships. Thus, people belonging to the same organization who share the same ideals and work for a common purpose are also a family. Anyone we

relate to, deeply and profoundly, we establish family ties with. Even though we have been blessed with one natural family, how many more we create is only limited by how involved we decide to get.

Taking a closer look at my life, I note that the closest people to me are my wife and two daughters. How did they assume such prominence? My wife was a total stranger until I met her and got to know her. My children did not even exist until they were born into my family. These two, spouse and children, came into my life and became its most important aspects. My wife became my family by invitation and through choice. My children, on the other hand, came in, though invited, but without much choice as to who they should be. Hence, there are two ways we can convert people into family: choice and invitation on the one hand and acceptance of what life brings our way on the other hand. We can learn to enlarge our circle of family and friends by exercising choice—selecting individuals to whom we want to relate—and by incorporating into our lives whomever life brings our way through circumstance.

From the above quote we learn how to form and expand our spiritual family at will.

WHO ART IN HEAVEN

Those who have not found the heaven below, will fail of it above. — Emily Dickinson

By invoking our Father "who is in heaven", we are implying that He is not here on earth. He is far away somewhere in heaven. Where exactly is heaven? Or more accurately, what is heaven? Since the Lord's Prayer is a hieroglyphic or sacred teaching, there are 4 levels at which we can understand the concepts presented in these teachings: the simple, the symbolic, the spiritual and the personal explanations.

The *simple* explanation

Heaven is a place where God resides or where souls go after death. This is where we can find saints and all the good people. According to this belief, not all souls go to heaven after death. Only the good ones do. (the believers?) Evildoers go to hell to suffer eternally. Some also believe in Purgatory where souls that are in between good and evil go to get purged and purified after which these souls ascend to heaven.

Obviously, believing in heaven and hell necessitates the belief in good and evil. This raises considerable difficulties that many simply ignore or gloss over. For example:

1. Since only the soul survives death, how can it be judged good or evil? Is it the soul or is it the body that commits good or evil while we live on earth?

2. If the soul is of God, how can it ever be evil?

3. If Heaven is where God is, does that mean He is not on earth?

4. Are all people equally good or equally evil to merit the same reward or punishment? Is there one heaven and one hell where everyone goes to or are there multiple heavens and hells based on the degree of goodness and evil?

5. Can eternal reward and eternal punishment be just for one lifetime of "sins" or "goodness"?

6. If heaven is a place somewhere out there, how come we never discovered it? We know what is out there in the sky. There are stars, solar systems, planets, galaxies, supernovas, meteors, comets, black holes and many other celestial bodies. If heaven is a place somewhere in the sky, where would it be?

7. If our Father is in heaven, how can He hear our prayers?

Heaven is often contrasted with earth. While earth is physical where "sin", corruption and imperfection reside, heaven is where perfection is. While earth is the domain of struggle, pain and suffering, heaven is where we experience none of these. While earth is enslavement to our appetites and imprisonment in a body, heaven is total freedom.

The *symbolic* and *allegorical* explanation

Heaven is not a place; rather it is an allegory, a metaphor for a particular state of being. People can be in heaven or hell while still alive and in a physical body. If people are in ecstasy, then they are in heaven. If, on the other hand, they are in agony, then they are in hell. Hence, both heaven and hell are states of mind. As John Milton said:

> *The mind is its own place, and in itself, can make heaven of Hell, and a hell of Heaven.*

The *spiritual* explanation

Heaven is perfection. It is the highest state of being where God, the epitome of perfection reigns supreme. It is what humans aspire to attain, a state they long to embody. Since, by my definition, God is **Love**, **Beauty** and **Joy**, then being in heaven is whenever we are overwhelmed by love, captivated by beauty and engulfed by joy. Anytime we experience the ideal of perfection in the form of love, beauty and joy, we are in heaven.

The *personal Gnostic* explanation

By stating in the Lord's Prayer, "**Our Father who art in Heaven**", we are implying that this Father is not on Earth or of earth. He is somewhere else, in heaven. Heaven is always contrasted with earth. We refer to them together as heaven and earth. These two states always go together. They are entangled.

While in English we use 4 words to describe where this Father is, in Syriac Aramaic it takes only one word with a preposition to describe this state. The Syriac Aramaic word for Heaven is "*shmayo.*" This word has other meanings such as sky, universe, and the entire cosmos. It is the Greek ***Ouranos.***

The words "who art in heaven" are not the best translation of the Syriac Aramaic "***d bashmayo***" which more accurately means "of heaven", "of the essence of Heaven", "that which belongs to heaven" or is "heavenly." It does not mean just *in* Heaven. The letter "d", the fourth letter of the alphabet, has several meanings, among them: in, among, with, at, to, into, on, upon, by, according to, for, because, and about.

Hence, our father is not necessarily in heaven as a physical place, but rather, our Father is heavenly or embodies the qualities of heaven. And what are these qualities? Perfection, expansion, and infinitude. Therefore, when something is of heaven, it is **expanded, unlimited** and **full of potential.** Conversely, when something is of earth, it is physical, **contracted, condensed, limited, and realized.**

Henceforth:

> While the body is of earth; the soul, mind and consciousness are of Heaven;
>
> While the particle is of earth; the wave is of Heaven;

While matter is of earth; energy and the field are of Heaven;

While expressions of ideas and ideals are of earth; ideas and ideals are of Heaven;

And while the practical and experiential are of earth; the theoretical and the imagined are of heaven.

Where is our Father?

Since by "our Father" we mean God, this Father must be everywhere—on earth, in heaven, in us and in everything. Everywhere means from the smallest atom to the entire universe. In other words, God the Father must be in all space and all matter. Space is always entangled with time and matter is condensed energy. How can God the Father be in everything and at all times?

The science of heaven and earth

Being is of two states: particle and wave. This is evident in the unit of light, the photon, which is a wavicle—expanded as wave and contracted as a particle. These two states are pervasive spanning from the humble electron to galaxies. When particles and elements come together, they combine their "particles" and their "waves." The particles form an ever-larger grouping of condensed bodies while the waves combine to form ever expanding fields.

We manifest our combined *particles* as the physical body which is condensed, tangible, and confined. The combination of our *waves* give rise to the fields is mind and consciousness. Our confined physical body is referred to as "Earth" while our expanded and intangible fields of mind and consciousness are denoted as "Heaven."

Anything that exists, exists as **vibration**. The rate of vibration determines how much of a **particle** or a **wave** something is. Those with the lowest rates of vibration manifest as matter and those with the highest as progressively expanded fields. Particles and waves always exist in specific, defined groups, bands or "quanta."

Within the human, the slowest rate of vibration is the physical body, the next higher vibration grouping is the astral body, then comes the spiritual body and finally, the highest rate of vibration belongs to our essence, the spark of divinity within which is our I AM.

Our I AM vibrates so intensely that we can never be aware of it. Our I AM is our soul which is of two parts: basic soul and epi-soul. Basic soul is what we start life with and is the same for everyone. Epi-soul is what we add to soul to make it our own individual unique soul. The more awareness, intelligence and "life" we imbue our epi-soul with, the more individual it becomes. Once it is mature, then we become conscious of our immortality. We remember who we are at all times.

Quantum theory and the various "heavens"

Is there one heaven or are there several "levels" of heavens? Is there one hell or are there multiple degrees of hells? Since heaven and hell are states of being, obviously, there must be several rungs to each.

Complex atoms can have multiple orbits for the electrons to move in, the more complex an atom, the larger the number of its orbits. Each orbit can occupy one and only one level. These levels are not continuous. They are discrete "quanta", each occupying one specific level and no other. An electron cannot move from one level to another. It must jump. By jumping, it does not traverse space. It simply manifests on the higher or the lower quanta, its new orbit.

Perhaps the various quanta in an atom are analogous to the various "levels of heaven" or "degrees of hell." When an electron jumps up to a higher orbit or quanta, it uses up energy. It is comparable to a human raising its level of consciousness. It requires the energy of effort. This must be provided by our thoughts, feelings, intentions and actions. When an electron drops to a lower orbit or quantum, it releases energy. It is as if a human descends to lower heavens or even to hell by pursuing temporary pleasures at the expense of its long-term well-being. It is all a matter of how well we use of minds and the choices we make. We can rise to a higher level or we can drop to a lower level depending on our choices. We are just like an atom where the level of our consciousness determines what orbit or quanta we occupy. How fascinating!

This knowledge places our fate squarely in our hands. Humans are gifted with free will. We must use it to further our goals and to ensure our happiness, wellbeing and the persistence of our individuality after we leave our physical bodies behind.

In summary

When we say: "Our Father who art in Heaven", "**Aboon d bashmayo**", what we are saying in essence is that we have two fathers, 2 sources or that we are dual in nature. All of us have the same Father who is in heaven, yet each of us has our own individual father who is on earth.

In other words, we are connected and separate, individual and collective, localized and dispersed. Through our earthly father, we are individual and material and of earth. Through our heavenly Father we are spiritual, connected to each other and are of heaven. Therefore, while heaven unites us, earth sets us apart.

We have a choice in how we identify ourselves. We can identify with our heavenly aspect or with our earthly counterpart. If we identify with our heavenly aspect, we are of heaven and are in heaven. If, on the other hand, we identify with our earthly aspect, the body with its needs, wants, and appetites, then we are on earth and are of earth.

Heaven is enduring. Earth is constantly in flux and changing. It is never the same from one moment to the next. If we identify with our heavenly part, we live in love, beauty and joy. We seek the treasures that do not spoil. If instead we identify with our earthly component, we live with struggle and uncertainly. We can be happy one day and miserable the next.

We come from heaven, and to heaven we return after we die. In heaven, we are perfect. Once we are born, we have made a decision to be on earth. On earth, we live by trial and error. We live and experience the results of our actions. We sow and we reap in accordance with the nature of the seeds we plant.

Here is yet another view of the meaning of heaven and earth from my book, **_A Passion for Living_**, *a path to meaning and joy:*

What we are is of earth, while who we are is of heaven. We are a visible, tangible, material body and an invisible, intangible animating factor. This is evident if we compare a living being to a corpse. The corpse does not have life. We are alive. We are sensitive, aware and can function. We live for as long as we are both, the life principle and the material through which this life principle expresses itself. Hence, we are changeless core and changing periphery. Individually, we are a breath exhaled as an emanation from our source. Yet, we remain anchored in our source as we extend out and undergo experiences as a unique individuality. At the source, we are the one who experiences. Away from the source, we are the experiences and the potential for more experiences. As we extend away from the source through our experiences of the world, we establish our individuality and identity. We become a unique soul personality.

Who and what we are, are two aspects of the same reality. Like matter and energy, they are interchangeable. What we are is of a lower rate of vibration than who we are, just as matter is of a lower vibratory rate than energy. Our core (who we are) vibrates at such a high rate that for all practical purposes, it stands still. What we are vibrates at varying rates. Our physical body vibrates at the lowest rate followed by our emotional, mental and finally the spiritual "body." Just as matter is constantly changing and assuming various forms and shapes so it is with what we are. It is constantly changing. Just as energy is the source from which matter forms and to which it returns, so it is with our body. It arises out of SELF, experiences, grows until it eventually becomes the SELF, thus returning to it.

HALLOWED BE THY NAME

The beginning of wisdom is calling things by their right names. —Confucius

To hallow is to consecrate, sanctify, bless, deify and to revere. "It is to make or set apart as holy". The word hallow is the same as the German word, "heiligen" which means to venerate, to respect, to honor greatly or to revere. Incidentally, Halloween is derived from to hallow as well. Halloween which falls on the evening of Oct. 31, is the All Hallows Eve or the eve of All Saints Day.

The Syriac Aramaic word for *"hallowed be"*, is: *"netkadash"*, derived from *"kadesh"* which means:

a) To cleanse and to make holy; to make sacred, to anoint and make "Christ-like";
b) To sanctify, or to make something the center-point of one's life.

The Arabic name for the city Jerusalem is "***Al Kudus***" from "***Kadesh***". In other words, Jerusalem is a holy city in the sense that it is central to people's lives and is considered to be a sanctified city, set aside as a holy city, a "***kudus***" or a "***Kadesh***".

Hence, when we say hallowed be thy name, we are setting the name of God aside as holy, pure, untouched and untouchable, divine and inspiring worship. But why are we hallowing the *name* of God instead of hallowing God directly? What is the name of God that are we hallowing?

There are many passages in the Bible where Jesus says do this or do that in my name. Why is that?

> *"Whoever receives one such child in my name receives me, ..." Matt 18:5*

And why is it that when Christians pray, they say: "In the name of the Father, the Son and the Holy Ghost"? Even Moslems, when they pray, they say: "***bsm ellah el raman el rahim***", in the name of God, the merciful, and the compassionate, or in the name of God, the Most Merciful and the Most Compassionate.

What is the name of God?

What exactly is the name of God that we are hallowing?

> *"I once heard of a mother who taught her child to say the Lord's Prayer every night before the child went to bed. So the mother, to make sure that her child was saying his prayers before he went to bed, one night she waited outside behind the door listening to her child say his prayers.*
>
> *The next day she confronted her child and said: "I am really proud of you. You learned your prayer well. I just have one question: Why were you*

praying to Harold instead of God?" To that the child replies: *"Isn't that God's name"? Because every time I hear you pray you say: "Our Father who art in Heaven, **Harold** be thy name!"*

The word for name in Syriac Aramaic is, **"shem"** and "thy name" would be
"shmokh". Does any secret power lie hidden in a name?

A name is a specialized form of a word and a word is a symbolic representation of a concept or an object. It is how we distinguish and separate one idea, object, or quality from another. From this we can see that to give something a name is to set it apart from all else, to give birth to it or to cause it to be, in the sense that it is individualized. Hence, to name is to define, to limit and to confine. It is to render the unlimited "heaven" into the limited or finite "earth".

A name houses a bundle of information. For example, if we are talking about a person by the name of Ella, initially the name Ella has little significance for us. As we get to know Ella and we share experiences, the name begins to become more and more significant in that it houses and represents a considerable amount of information and memories. It becomes a repository of our shared experiences.

A name is defined as **"A word or words by which an entity is designated and distinguished from others".** This is what a name means to us. But for the ancients, a name was much more than a designation. A name had power and magic.

The following are a few selected paragraphs from, **"The Women's Encyclopedia of Myths and Secrets,"** *a wonderful resource book by Barbara Walker.*

For the purposes of magic and religion, the name of anything was considered identical with the thing itself, a spiritual "handle" by which the thing or the supernatural being could be manipulated. Children and primitives seldom distinguish clearly between the reality and the name of an object.

Each Egyptian's soul-name, the ren, was breathed by a mother on her child as it was first put to her breast; therefore the Goddess of soul-names was Renenet, who governed lactation. Without its ren, the child would have no identity and would not be allowed to eat. Even the gods needed mothers to give them names, otherwise they would pine away and die. The same belief is found in India: the "thousand-eyed god" named Existence cried immediately after he was born, "Give me a name, for without a name I will not eat food."

The great importance attached to names goes back to the earliest ages, and probably bears a profound psychological relationship to the human animal's unique ability to verbalize. Names were confused with souls almost everywhere. Egyptians said "To speak the name of the dead is to make them live again." Tomb inscriptions begged passers-by to speak the name of the entombed, to give "the breath of life to him who has vanished." " No greater harm could be done to an Egyptian than to erase the carving or writing of his name. To destroy the very letters meant destruction of the soul.

Precedents older than civilization evolved the idea that forces of creation and destruction could be activated by pronouncing a divine name. The Mother of Gods controlled her offspring by knowledge of their secret names. Early priestly theory proposed that these secret names could be learned by human beings, who could then control the gods with them. Brahman priests claimed to control the gods' actions with mantras incorporating the divine names. Some of their lore was embodied in the Upanishads, which means "secret names."[32] The name of the Amida Buddha was so powerful that a priest could send himself or any other man to the Western Paradise immediately only by uttering it.

The Islamic Allah was even better equipped, with ninety-nine secret names. Moslems claimed he would be compelled to answer any prayer if all these names were pronounced. Allah himself was called "the Essential Name," originally the milk-giving Goddess Al-Lat. Pious Moslems invoked Allah's name before sexual intercourse **so no** evil spirit could enter the womb and beget an evil child.

Both Moslems and Christians inherited Jewish name-magic and believed that all sorts of miracles could be worked by invoking the name of God or the name of Christ, to say nothing of their secret names. In the Middle Ages it was believed that any priest could absolutely compel God to do whatever was asked, by conducting a Mass of the Holy Spirit which mentioned God's secret name. The powers of God's name were explained by Henry Morley as follows:
Whoever knows the true pronunciation of the name Jehovah—the name from which all other divine names in the world spring as the branches from a tree, the name that binds together the sephiroth—

*whoever has **that** in his mouth has the world in his mouth. When it is spoken angels are stirred by the waves of sound. It rules all creatures, works all miracles, it commands all the inferior names of deity which are borne by the several angels that in heaven govern the respective nations of the earth.*

*Both Jewish and Christian Gnostics focused on the power of divine names to bring about healing, exorcism, absolution, and salvation. In the **Pistis Sophia**, Jesus told his disciples to "hide the mystery" of a great Name that could dissolve evil and "blot out all sins, done knowing or not knowing." According to the Gospels, this was the esoteric secret that Jesus concealed from all but his intimates. The masses were not told, "lest at any time they should be converted, and their sins should be forgiven them" (Mark 4:11), indicating that early Christianity like other mystery-religions addressed itself to a favored few. Jesus gave the disciples his secret name, which had power to exorcise, when he said "In my name shall they cast out devils" (Mark 16:17). Seventy of his followers told him, "Lord, even the devils are subject unto us through thy name" (Luke 10:17). Origen said Jesus' name had "expelled myriads of evil spirits from the souls and bodies of men." According to the Enchiridion, the powers of Jesus's name were so far-reaching that it was hard to see how anything could possibly go wrong in a world where it was spoken:*
O sacred Name, Name which strengthens the heart of man. Name of life, of salvation, of joy, precious Name, resplendent, glorious, agreeable Name, which fortifies the sinner. Name which saves, conserves, leads and rules all... wheresoever the most sweet Name of Jesus is pronounced ...

the demons take flight, every knee is bent, all temptations, even the worst, are scattered, all infirmities are healed, all disputes and conflicts between the world, the flesh and the devil are ended, and the soul is filled with every heavenly delight.'"

The holy names were not merely symbols. Words spoken "in the name of Jesus" or "in the name of the Father, Son, and Holy Ghost" were supposed to have absolute efficacy in expelling
demons from altars, candles, fonts, even church hassocks, just as Egyptian hekau could expel demons from a pyramid. Certainly man never invented a weapon easier to use against the evil powers that he felt threatening him on all sides. Nothing could induce him to abandon it, then or now.

From a number of passages in various Egyptian texts, it is evident that Isis was thought to possess great skill in magic. One of her great feats was recorded in the myth of Ra. Since most mythologies believe that to possess the true name of a god was to have power over that god, many deities had more than one name; that is, one by which they were generally known and another, which might be called the real name, that was kept secret lest it come into the hands of an enemy and be used against them. Isis once tried to make Ra reveal to her his greatest and most secret name.

"Cannot I by means of the sacred name of God make myself mistress of the earth and become a goddess of like rank and power to Ra in heaven and upon earth?" she asked herself.

Using her magical skill, she made a venomous reptile out of dust mixed with Ra's spittle, and by uttering certain words of power over the reptile made it sting Ra as he passed through the heavens. The sun god, who was at the point of death, was forced to reveal his hidden name. Satisfied at last, Isis recited an incantation to drain the poison from Ra's limbs, and the god recovered.

What does all this mean?

We know that knowing the name of a deity is important. But how can we know what this name is and how to pronounce it correctly?

First, we need to find out if God has one name, 72 names, 99 names, or an infinite number of names? In my book, __A Passion for Living__, *a path to meaning and joy,* I explain that there are three levels from which we can view life and glean an understanding of what it is. I go on to state that:

1. The first level is that of the physical manifestation, the product;
2. The second level is that of the blueprint; and
3. The third level is that of the architect, the author, and the creator.

Using the same approach, we can state that there are three types of names for God corresponding to the 3 levels of being and functioning:

1. An __*obvious*__ name which corresponds to the manifest product level;
2. A __*hidden*__ name which corresponds to the blueprint level; and
3. A __*secret*__ name which corresponds to the

architect, author and creator level.

Knowing God's obvious name

The obvious name is the one by which a thing or a person is known by. We give people and animals names so that we may distinguish between one and another. In Genesis 2:19-20 it is stated:

> So out of the ground the LORD God formed every animal of the field and every bird of the air, and brought them to the man to see what he would call them; and whatever the man called every living creature, that was its name. The man gave names to all cattle, and to the birds of the air, and to every animal of the field; but for the man there was not found a helper as his partner.

Everybody has an obvious name. This is our given name. God, too, has an obvious name. This name varies from religion to religion and changes over time. Some of God's obvious names are: God, Allah, Brahma, Elohim, El Shaddai, Adoni, the ancient of days and so forth.

Anyone can know and utter the obvious name. It is devoid of any power or magic. This is the name which most use when they pray and think of when *hallowing* the name of God. Using the obvious name of God is usually done when one prays from the lips and as a routine.

Knowing God's hidden name

The hidden name of God has power and magic to it if we know what it is and learn to "pronounce" it correctly. Even though this name is hidden, it is not secret. In other words, this name is only a mystery and hidden from us, if we do not know where to look for it. Once we know where to look for it, it becomes obvious and we see it everywhere.

The secret to knowing the Hidden Name of God lies in a passage in the Gospel according to Matthew.

Judgment of the Nations:

> *"When the Son of Man comes in his glory, and all the angels with him, then he will sit on the throne of his glory. All the nations will be gathered before him, and he will separate people one from another as a shepherd separates the sheep from the goats, and he will put the sheep at his right hand and the goats at the left. Then the king will say to those at his right hand, 'Come, you that are blessed by my Father, inherit the kingdom prepared for you from the foundation of the world; for I was hungry and you gave me food, I was thirsty and you gave me something to drink, I was a stranger and you welcomed me, I was naked and you gave me clothing, I was sick and you took care of me, I was in prison and you visited me.' Then the righteous will answer him, 'Lord, when was it that we saw you hungry and gave you food, or thirsty and gave you something to drink? And when was it that we saw you a stranger and welcomed you, or naked and gave you clothing? And when was it that we saw you sick or in prison and visited you?' And the king will answer them, 'Truly I tell you, just as you did it to one of the least of these who are members of my family, you did it to me.' Then he will say to those at his left hand, 'You that are accursed, depart from me into the eternal fire prepared for the devil and his angels; for I was hungry and you gave me no food, I was thirsty and you gave me nothing to*

> drink, I was a stranger and you did not welcome me, naked and you did not give me clothing, sick and in prison and you did not visit me.' Then they also will answer, 'Lord, when was it that we saw you hungry or thirsty or a stranger or naked or sick or in prison, and did not take care of you?' Then he will answer them, 'Truly I tell you, just as you did not do it to one of the least of these, you did not do it to me.' And these will go away into eternal punishment, but the righteous into eternal life." Matt 25:31-46

What we learn from this passage is that we can never know God or His hidden name directly. **We can only know God's hidden name by proxy, as each other. In other words, each being is one of God's hidden names.** You and I are each a hidden name of God. This name is already uttered as you and me and that is why we cannot utter this hidden name in the physical sense. We can, however, hallow it by honoring each other.

The above passage makes it clear that each person represents one of the hidden names of God. The word *person* is composed of two syllables:

> Per which means through;
> Son from "sona" which means sound.

In other words, a person is someone through whom a sound is expressed or uttered. In other words, each person is a hidden word, a sound or a name of God. We are each a specific person, a unique individual, a special utterance, a vessel (name) through which God expresses Him/Herself.

How to honor God's hidden name
An exercise

This exercise can be practiced with a family member or anyone else. It can be done silently or by uttering the words aloud.

Sit facing the person you are to honor and look into their eyes. Feel love in your heart for this individual and then say:

I, (your name), now know that you, (the person's name), are one of God's hidden names. If I know you, I will know one of God's miraculous manifestations. Knowing you is uttering and manifesting one of God's hidden names. By hallowing you, (the person's name), I am hallowing the hidden name of God that you are a manifestation of.

Take a few moments and bathe yourself in this attitude and feeling.

This exercise can be done anytime and with anyone, not only people, but animals, trees, or anything we choose. It is empowering and transformative. Making a habit of doing this exercise secretly and routinely will change not only us, but the world as well.

The greatest of all commandments

When Christ was asked what was the single most important or the greatest of all the commandments, this is what He said:

> *"Teacher, which commandment in the law is the greatest?" He said to him, "'You shall love the Lord*

> *your God with all your heart, and with all your soul, and with all your mind.' This is the greatest and first commandment. And a second is like it: 'You shall love your neighbor as yourself.' On these two commandments hang all the law and the prophets."*
> *Matthew 22:36-40*

The reason this is the greatest commandment is because ***it reveals the hidden name of God.*** Notice that the greatest commandment is a dual commandment because we can never do one without doing the other. We can never love God directly. We must do it through loving our neighbor and once we love our neighbor, we have automatically loved God. There is no distinction. Doing one leads directly to the other instantly. (Our neighbor is anyone and everyone we encounter in the process of living).

Knowing God's secret name

The God of the ancient Hebrews had an ineffable name, a name that cannot be expressed, described or uttered. This ineffable name is known as the Tetragrammaton consisting of the four Hebrew letters ***yod, he, vau, he (YHWH).*** This name was so secret and holy that it could not be pronounced, except once a year, and only by the high priest. These four Hebrew letters are usually transliterated as YHWH or JHVH (Yahweh or Jehovah) and used as a proper biblical name for God.

Yehweh in Syriac Aramaic means **"*To Be*"** or **"*Being*"** while EHWEH (aleph, he, wow, aleph) means **"*I AM*"**.

How can YHWH or JEHOVA be God's secret name if we already know what it means? What is so secret about ***"Being or I AM"***?

Growing up as a child in the Middle East, I was very confused as to why God had to be three in one or one in three. Why the trinity? Why not simply one God who is indivisible and not sharing its essence and power?

As I grew up, I realized that if God were one and all was God, there could be no contrast, comparison, or any activity. Without activity there could be no change and without change there could be no being. Hence, God cannot be one as a single, homogeneous unit.

God could not be a duality either if these 2 were inert which would be useless. Having 2 identical units that remain separate and neutral and never interact, there would still be no change or activity.

The only way we can have change, transformation, newness and activity is if there were 2 and these 2 were unlike each other. An active component with "masculine qualities" and a passive component with "feminine qualities" who interact to give birth to a third new entity, an offspring or a "child" containing qualities from both. This is why trinity is a must.

Trinity is a spiritual law known as the ***Law of the Triangle***. Not only God is a trinity but so are we, and in fact all of being. Please refer to my book: ***Know Yourself, Love Yourself and Express Yourself***, *a spiritual guide to intentional living* for more details.

The trinity of God is the masculine and active (the Father), the feminine and passive (The Mother of the Holy Spirit), and the resultant offspring. (the Son or the Child).

We are a trinity as well—physical, astral and spiritual.

Our mind is a trinity of conscious, subconscious and superconscious.

And just as there are 3 levels of knowing and pronouncing the names of God, The **Obvious**, the **Hidden** and the **Secret names**, there are three levels to experience reality as well.

1. The first level corresponds to the obvious, the *physical reality* as we experience it around us. At this level, reality is four dimensional, governed by space, time and the laws of physics. This is the realm of constant change, transformation and becoming. At this level, there is past, present, and future. There is here, there, now, and then. This level is characterized as the Level of **becoming and corresponds with the obvious name of God**.

2. The second level corresponds to *the hidden reality*. This is the level of organized energy and quantum fields. This is where we can use the advanced faculties of mind such as will, intention, and visualization to create mental blueprints, mental genes, and mental seeds. Even though at this stage there is change, everything is connected in an ocean of energy or quantum fields. At this level interconnectedness is evident. This level is characterized as that of **causation, formation and creation** and corresponds with the Hidden name of God.

3. The third level corresponds to *the secret reality*. This is the level of awareness, intelligence and

changeless *being*. This is the realm of the *I AM*. This level corresponds with the secret name of God, ehweh, yehweh, or Jehowa and I AM.

Just knowing these three names of God, the obvious, the hidden and the secret names, is not enough. We must learn how to hollow, pronounce and express these names so we can unravel their magic and benefit from their power.

Hallowing the 3 names of God—"netkadash shmokh!"

1. It is easy to hallow the obvious name of God. All we have to do is say the word God, Allah, Brahma, Elohim, El Shaddai, Adoni and so forth. This is exactly what most do. Uttering this name or hallowing God by simply saying: "***Hallowed be Thy Name***" is empty, sterile and has no power to move or impact anything. Most people use the obvious name of God out of habit and without giving it much thought. A few even use this name as a curse such as when they say, "God damn you".

2. It is more difficult to hallow the hidden name of God. To do this, we must become aware of others. We must go beyond our selfish ego and care for others genuinely. To utter the hidden name of God, we must feel love and compassion toward another. We must see our interrelatedness and our ultimate unity. We are not only connected to every other human, but to all life forms. In fact, we are inseparable from our planet, the solar system and the entire

cosmos. We can use the previous simple exercise to utter the hidden name of God when we are with other people. We can use this exercise with all other beings as well. Uttering the hidden name of God by honoring the God in another is a powerful way of hallowing the name of God. It can transform everyone involved.

3. The most powerful way to hallow the name of God is to utter God's secret name. To do this, we must not *do*, but we must **_become_** and this is where **I AM** or EHWH or BEING and JEHOVA come into play. From this level of functioning, we do not honor another; we walk in their shoes. We do not love; we become love. We do not see; we become that which we are to see. We do not touch; we sense our unity. At this state of being, all the Self; there is no other. Our self and the other selves are mere aspects or expressions of the one and only Self. From this level of functioning, we manifest the Christ consciousness. And as the Christ consciousness, we can say: I AM light, I AM life, I AM Love, I AM the way, and I AM the resurrection.

This "I", however, is not me small self, or the ego. It is the big "I" which encompasses ALL. And when we function from this level, whatever we are, so is everything else. In other words, we experience the world as a reflection of who we are. From this vantage point, any thought we think, any feeling we sense, any intention or thought we entertain is a blueprint. It is a fertilized egg or a seed dropped in fertile soil. It is only a matter of time before it manifests as a physical reality.

Since we are in the image of God, we too have three names: **obvious, hidden,** and **secret**. Our obvious name is our given name, our hidden name is our life's mission, while our secret name is our soul name, our special imprint that identifies us as a unique individual. This is what the ancient Egyptians called the *"ren"*.

This is also why Christ had three names as well: Jesus (obvious), Messiah (hidden), and Emmanuelle (secret). Knowing hidden and secret names are empowering, enlightening and transformative. For more information about this subject, please refer to my book: ***Know Yourself, Love Yourself and Express Yourself, a spiritual guide to intentional living.***

Even though we are separating God into a trinity and the name of God into three types: obvious, hidden and secret, everything is interconnected, related, and ultimately of one essence. As Spinoza says:

> *"All the cosmos is a single substance of which we are a part. God is not an external manifestation, but everything that is".*

THY KINGDOM COME

There can be no Kingdom of God in the world without the Kingdom of God in our hearts. — Albert Schweitzer

Now that we have the attention of our heavenly Father, what is it that we want to say, ask for, or express? What do we want to achieve through this sacred contact?

Thy Kingdom come! *"Teeteh Malkutokh."*

We are asking for the Father's kingdom to come, to manifest here on earth. What is this kingdom?

There are two types of kingdoms mentioned in the New Testament: Kingdom of God and kingdom of heaven. Are these different or the same? We say *"thy"* kingdom come! meaning the Father's kingdom. This father is God and He is in heaven. Therefore, the kingdom of heaven and the kingdom of God are one and the same. Here are 2 verses to show that this is so.

Kingdom of heaven

> *Repent, for the kingdom of heaven is at hand.*
> *Matthew 3:2*

Kingdom of God

> *But strive first for the kingdom of God and his righteousness and all these things will be given to you as well. Matthew 6:33*

What exactly is this kingdom and what do we mean when we say, *"Thy Kingdom Come?"* As before, there are 4 ways we can interpret sacred writings: simple, symbolic, spiritual and personal.

The simple interpretation

In the simple interpretation, *"Thy kingdom come"* alludes to the second coming of Christ where He is expected to come in His glory and literally rule over the earth. For those who espouse this interpretation, the first coming took place in Bethlehem some 2000 years ago. Even though the second coming has not yet taken place, the time for it, supposedly, is near. The believers in this point of view have been looking for signs to determine when the second coming will take place. The hope was that it would be soon after the establishment of the state of Israel, but that did not happen. Even though no one knows exactly when the second coming will take place, there are signs to look for to know when the time is near and the end of times is at hand.

Here are some verses from the New Testament on what to look for:

The Coming of the Son of Man

> *There will be signs in the sun, the moon, and the stars, and on the earth distress among nations confused by the roaring of the sea and the waves. People will faint from fear and foreboding of what is coming upon the world, for the powers of the heavens will be shaken. Then they will see 'the Son of Man coming in a cloud' with power and great glory. Now when these things begin to take place, stand up and raise your heads, because your redemption is drawing near. Luke 21: 25-28*

The Lesson of the Fig Tree

> *Then he told them a parable: "Look at the fig tree and all the trees; as soon as they sprout leaves you can see for yourselves and know that summer is already near. So also, when you see these things taking place, you know that the kingdom of God is near. Truly I tell you, this generation will not pass away until all things have taken place. Heaven and earth will pass away, but my words will not pass away. Luke 21: 29-33*

Exhortation to Watch

> *Be on guard so that your hearts are not weighed down with dissipation and drunkenness and the worries of this life, and that day does not catch you unexpectedly, like a trap. For it will come upon all who live on the face of the whole earth. Be alert at all times, praying that you may have the strength to escape all these things that will take place, and to stand before the Son of Man. Luke 21: 34-36*

To believe in a literal second coming of Jesus, one must

account for the various inconsistencies, such as verse 32 that states:

> *Truly I tell you, this generation will not pass away until all things have taken place. Luke 21:32*

In other words, Christ was talking about the immediate future not the far future. He was talking about His generation. Since this has passed and there was no second coming, the literal interpretation cannot be what Christ had in mind.

The symbolic interpretation

The second way to interpret the second coming of Christ is to consider it as symbolic, an allegory, a figure of speech and as a parable. It is easy to do this since Christ used stories, allegories and parables to explain what he had in mind.

When Christ taught us to ask for the Kingdom to come, by saying, "***Thy kingdom come***", He did not mean it as a physical kingdom with a king who is Jesus. For when Jesus was asked if He was a king, He stated that his kingdom was not from this world. In other words, it was not a physical kingdom. That is why he requested his disciples to go out into the world and proclaim the kingdom of God or the kingdom of Heaven was attainable and is at hand. This is the good news that the disciples carried to the world proclaiming the kingdom of Heaven is at hand and that *anyone* can attain it.

> *And he said to them, "Go into all the world and proclaim the gospel to the whole creation." Mark 16:15*

The spiritual interpretation

The third way to interpret *"Thy kingdom come"*, is to look for its spiritual meaning. The spiritual kingdom is where the rule of God is the law and where the will of God is expressed and established on earth. This is when there is peace on earth, everyone lives by love, is compassionate and radiates good will towards everyone else.

Jesus is the example of one who embodied this kingdom by living its tenets. His life was an example of someone who had attained the highest level of consciousness—the Christ Consciousness. Jesus was the prototype, the example of what we can be and how we should live. He stated that what He did, we can do as well, but only as children of God. Anyone who brings light to a darkened world (enlightenment), food (nurturing) to the hungry, clothes (education and culture) to the naked, water (spiritual insights) to the thirsty, and especially peace where there is war, is a child of God.

> *Blessed are the peacemakers, for they shall be called sons of God. Matt 5:9*

In the process of growth and maturation, humanity has known several **"Sons of God"** or spiritual teachers who appeared at auspicious times to lead humanity one step closer to establishing the Kingdom of Heaven on Earth. Among them are Prometheus, Hermes, Akhenaton, Zoroaster, Krishna, Lao-Tzu, the Buddha, Mohammed, and Baha-o-llah. The spiritual interpretation emphasizes that whoever attains enlightenment or the Christ Consciousness, establishes the kingdom of God in their lives and on Earth.

The personal interpretation

The fourth and final way to interpret *"Thy Kingdom come"* is the personal point of view. By asking for the kingdom of God to come, we are admitting that this kingdom is not here yet, else why would we ask for it to come? Before we can fully comprehend the significance of what we are asking for, we must reconcile three different versions as to when the kingdom of God will come: It is already here; it will be manifesting shortly; or will it be in the future?

Kingdom of God is already here and within us

> *Once Jesus was asked by the Pharisees when the kingdom of God was coming, and he answered, "The kingdom of God is not coming with things that can be observed; nor will they say, 'Look, here it is!' or 'There it is!' For, in fact, the kingdom of God is among (or within) you." Luke17: 20-21*

Some believe that this verse refers to Christ and that He was the Kingdom of God and that He was talking about Himself. However, in Mark 9:1 and in Luke 9:27, we read that the coming of the Kingdom of Heaven is not here yet, but is imminent.

Kingdom of God will manifest shortly

> *And he said to them, "Truly I tell you, there are some standing here who will not taste death until they see that the kingdom of God has come with power." Mark 9:1*

> *But I tell you truly, there are some standing here who will not taste death until they see the*

> *kingdom of God." Luke 9:27*

Kingdom of God will manifest in the future

> *And this gospel of the kingdom will be proclaimed throughout the whole world as a testimony to all nations, and then the end will come. Matt 24:14*

Which is it? Is the Kingdom of God already here, is it coming shortly or will it be coming in the future? And if it is already here, why would Christ teach us to pray asking for this kingdom to come?

All three statements are true. The kingdom of God is already here, it will be coming shortly and it might take a long time for it to manifest fully. How can this be? This is not a paradox once we understand what the Kingdom of God is.

Christ told us what this kingdom is. Unfortunately, He used parables and parables hide the inner meaning of the story. For a full explanation of what these parables hide, please refer to my book, **_The Secret Teachings of Christ, based on the parables._**

Here are the parables regarding the Kingdom of Heaven:

> *He put before them another parable: "The kingdom of heaven may be compared to someone who sowed good seed in his field; but while everybody was asleep, an enemy came and sowed weeds among the wheat, and then went away. So when the plants came up and bore grain, then the weeds appeared as well. And the slaves of the householder came and said to him, 'Master, did you not sow good seed in your field? Where,*

> then, did these weeds come from?' He answered, 'An enemy has done this.' The slaves said to him, 'Then do you want us to go and gather them?' But he replied, 'No; for in gathering the weeds you would uproot the wheat along with them. Let both of them grow together until the harvest; and at harvest time I will tell the reapers, Collect the weeds first and bind them in bundles to be burned, but gather the wheat into my barn.'"
> Matt 13:24-30

In this parable there is a field containing both weed and wheat. The owner plants good seeds (wheat) while the enemy plants bad seeds (weed). The explanation of this parable is given in the Parable of the Sower. This is where Christ explains the hidden meaning of the parable. He says:

> Hear then the parable of the sower. When anyone hears the word of the kingdom and does not understand it, the evil one comes and snatches away what is sown in the heart; this is what was sown on the path. As for what was sown on rocky ground, this is the one who hears the word and immediately receives it with joy; yet such a person has no root, but endures only for a while, and when trouble or persecution arises on account of the word, that person immediately falls away. As for what was sown among thorns, this is the one who hears the word, but the cares of the world and the lure of wealth choke the word, and it yields nothing. But as for what was sown on good soil, this is the one who hears the word and understands it, who indeed bears fruit and yields,

> *in one case a hundredfold, in another sixty, and in another thirty. Mat 13:18-23*

The Kingdom of God then is the field where we sow seeds. This field is our lives, specifically our hearts and minds. And that is why I call myself a Cultivator of the Mind. I am a cultivator of the mind and I help hasten the coming of the Kingdom of Heaven— peace, cooperation and the maximizing of the human potential.

What we sow in the field of the mind and the heart are seeds. These seeds could be "wheat" or "weed." The seeds are our thoughts, intentions, what we fear, what we hope for and what we desire. Therefore, the Kingdom of God is the mind/heart where the seeds in it are the "words" and where the "plants" growing in this field yield fruit that reflect what was sown. What we allow to grow in our mind/heart determines what we experience in our daily lives.

Each of us has a unique field based on our understanding and the level of our consciousness. This is reflected in the experiences we have and the quality of our lives. We are each unique not only in our physical aspects such our genes, fingerprints, and retinal configuration, but more importantly, in the type of field we are cultivating. In most, this field (mind/heart) is fallow, ignored and uncultivated and where **"weed"** and **"wheat"** grow randomly.

Resolving the conflicts
1. The Kingdom is already here

Since Christ expressed the Kingdom of Heaven by the

example of His life and since His consciousness was as high as it gets, He was the Kingdom of Heaven as manifest on earth. Thus, wherever He is, there also is the Kingdom of Heaven for He is that Kingdom, that state of being, that consciousness. ***Hence, the Kingdom is already here and manifest as the Christ Consciousness.***

2. Witnessing the coming of the Kingdom

Anyone who attains the Christ Consciousness witnesses the coming of the Kingdom of God in their own lives. Thus, anyone living in the days of Christ who attained the Christ Consciousness, (has not tasted death) has witnessed the coming of the Kingdom of Heaven. This could include his disciples and a few others.

3. The Kingdom is yet to come

Many will attain the Christ Consciousness and manifest the kingdom of Heaven in their lives in the future. It is a matter of time. When a majority of people attain this consciousness, that will be the Second Coming of Christ. His consciousness will then rule Earth through our individual Christ Consciousness that we would have assumed and incorporated as our modus operandi.

This is how the Kingdom of Heaven can be among us, will descend in the near future, or it in the far future. It depends on when we attain the Christ Consciousness. As we live, learn and mature, we should endeavor to raise our consciousness to the highest level attainable, what we term Christ or Cosmic Consciousness. Once at this level, the second coming would have taken place and the

Kingdom of Heaven would manifest on earth. And this is what we are asking when we say, *"Thy kingdom come!"*

Royalty

A kingdom is the domain of a king or a queen, of royalty. There are two types of royalties—material and spiritual. Material royalty is where a physical king or queen rules over us, their subjects. Materia royals are viewed as better, loftier, wealthier, more powerful, elite and wise. This creates separation. Royals rule and the rest are ruled. The royals are the masters and the rest are their subjects.

Spiritual royalty is different. It is for every individual. If God is King and a spark of the divine is in me, in you, and in all, then in essence, we are all consecrated, divine and royal. In our kingdom, all subjects are aligned to the will of the divine within us. Our Higher Self, the I AM, is the royal while the subjects are our thoughts, feelings and the ego. When this spiritual kingdom manifests in our lives, the ego takes backstage. Individuals are not compared as better or worse. Each individual is a different aspect of the same divinity. Each is another royal to be appreciated and looked upon with awe, wonder and amazement.

Thy Kingdom Come! is an invitation for the realization of the divine in all of us to manifest in our daily lives. The kingdom of God is a kingdom where love rules. When we greet another, we need to look into each other's eyes (souls) and say; "Namaste!" This customary Hindu greeting recognizes and honors the divine light in each and every one – the God in me greets the God in you.

When the Kingdom of Heaven is established in our lives, then we realize that we are the king or the queen of our kingdom. Our words, thoughts and intentions are the law. We have the power, the status, and the authority of a monarch. We are the Light of our world! We are The Way of our kingdom! We are the Truth, the Life, and the Resurrection of our lives.

The number 4

The number 4 is symbolic for the square, solidity, stability and balance. This is why there are many references to number 4 in ancient literature. We live in space/time; 3 dimensions for space and 1 for time. There are four cardinal points: East, West, North and South. We have four gospels: Matthew, Luke. Mark and John. There were 4 rivers flowing through the Garden of Eden. The ancients also had the four elements: Earth, Water, Air and Fire. To attain the Kingdom of Heaven in our lives, we need to master our physical body, our mind, our emotions and the ego. We need to function from our Higher Self.

The ancients called the physical body, Earth; the astral body, Water; the spiritual body, Air; and they called the soul, Fire. Additionally, they symbolized the individual with a lit candle. The candle has 4 aspects:

1. The solid wax which they termed **Earth** and associated it with the physical body;
2. The molten wax which they termed **Water** and associated it with the emotions;
3. The air consumed by the candle which they termed **Air** and associated it with the mind; and
4. The fire of the candle which they termed **Fire** and associated it with the soul.

Exercise

Whether physically or in your imagination, find yourself in a green pasture. Lie down with your arms extended. Orient yourself so that your head points to the East, your feet point to the West, your right arm extends towards the North and your left arm points to the South.

Close your eyes, take a few deep breaths and relax your body. With each inhalation, imagine that you are taking in the vital life force from the atmosphere. Hold your breath and imagine that you are absorbing the vitality from the air and distributing it throughout your body. Exhale slowly. With each exhalation, let go of all tensions, worries and accumulated toxins. Once fully relaxed, focus on the figure of the cross you have formed with your body.

Place yourself in the center of the cross. Imagine that you reside at this center. This is where you operate from. This is where your source is.

Visualize Christ on the cross. His Consciousness is at the center of the cross. Christ has conquered His lower self: His physical body, His mind, His emotions and His ego. We need to do the same.

Focus your attention on your right arm, the North, associated with Earth. This represents your physical body. Review your appetites and cravings. Resolve to master them through sublimation.

Next, focus your attention on your left arm, the South, associated with Water. This represents your emotions. Review your feelings and resolve to replace the negative with the positive, hate with love, fear with courage, envy with appreciation.

Next, focus your attention on your feet, the West, associated with Air. This represents your thoughts. Review your habits, attitudes, expectations and beliefs. Let go of what is no longer needed. Focus instead on that which is uplifting, enlivening and empowering.

Finally, focus your attention on your head, the East, associated with Fire. This represents your ego and the lower self. Resolve to let go of the ego. Determine to allow the Kingdom of Heaven to manifest in your life. Assume the qualities of Christ: love, compassion, acceptance and humility.

To attain the Kingdom of Heaven, we must become the rulers of our internal world. We must evaluate our thoughts, refine our emotions and carefully select the words we utter and the actions we take. We must put our egos behind us and allow our consciousness to rise and soar. As we do, our hearts soften, we begin to see clearly and hear the Voice Within distinctly. Progressively, we reach for and eventually attain the Christ Consciousness. When we do, we become the King or the Queen of our own personalized Kingdom of Heaven. We transform from being the son of Man to being the Son of God.

> *As children of Earth, as Sons of man, we use our bodies, emotions, and minds to gratify our senses, attain control over others, satisfy our desires and to compete for survival.*

As children of God, we employ our bodies, emotions, minds, and intuition to further the objectives of our soul, to live our life's mission and to aid humanity progress toward maturity.

THY WILL BE DONE ON EARTH, AS IT IS IN HEAVEN

There are scores of thousands of human insects who are ready at a moment's notice to reveal the will of God on every possible subject. — George Bernard Shaw

Perhaps this statement is the most parroted section of the Lord's Prayer. How many know what the will of God in heaven is? How can we ask to have it manifest on earth when we do not know what it is? By stating, "thy will be done on earth as it is in heaven", "nhweh sbyonokh aykano d bashmayo oph b aroh" in Syriac Aramaic, we are assuming that there must be two wills, one in heaven and one on earth. If there is another will on earth other than the will of God, whose will is it?

Once more, we will consider the 4 levels of interpretation.

The simple interpretation

We are asking for God's will to be expressed on earth as it is in heaven. Many view heaven as the domain of God where His will is established, while the earth is the domain of the Devil and that the Devil is in charge on Earth and that his will dominates earth. This may be construed from the story of Job where the Devil is given total freedom to do as he pleases with the people on earth:

> Now there was a day when the sons of God came to present themselves before the LORD, and Satan also came among them. The LORD said to Satan, "From where have you come?" Satan answered the LORD and said, "From going to and fro on the earth, and from walking up and down on it." And the LORD said to Satan, "Have you considered my servant Job, that there is none like him on the earth, a blameless and upright man, who fears God and turns away from evil?" Then Satan answered the LORD and said, "Does Job fear God for no reason? Have you not put a hedge around him and his house and all that he has, on every side? You have blessed the work of his hands, and his possessions have increased in the land. But stretch out your hand and touch all that he has, and he will curse you to your face." And the LORD said to Satan, "Behold, all that he has is in your hand. Only against him do not stretch out your hand." So Satan went out from the presence of the LORD. Job 1:6-12

The assumption is that the Devil establishes his will on earth through people. When individuals carry out evil acts, it is assumed that, **"the Devil made them do it."** Yet, when we are faced with events beyond our control such as hurricanes, tornados or earthquakes that destroy homes and lives, we explain these as "acts of God."

Natural events are not "acts of God." They are merely the ramifications of natural laws. God does not interfere in our daily affairs for that would rob us of our freedom of choice and the right to make mistakes and learn from them. When people experience pain and suffering, it is never the will of God for us to suffer. Hence, we mostly live our lives expressing our will instead of God's will. Unfortunately, we mostly express the will of our ego, rather than the will of our Higher Self.

The symbolic interpretation

The symbolic interpretation assumes that the will of God in Heaven embodies peace, harmony, goodness, love, justice, compassion, and caring. We are asking that these same qualities be expressed on earth, hopefully, through us.

The spiritual interpretation

The spiritual interpretation of, "thy will be done on earth as it is in heaven", is a reference to the ancient law of correspondence that states: *As Above, So Below*. In other words, earth is a reflection of heaven or the visible world is a reflection of the invisible world and that whatever is on earth has its counterpart in heaven. Conversely, whatever is in heaven has its counterpart on earth. In other words, the microcosm is analogous to the macrocosm. An example of this would be the revolution of the electrons around the nucleus of an atom being comparable to the rotation of the planets around the sun.

The personal interpretation

To understand **the personal meaning** *of, "thy will be done on earth, as it is in heaven",* we must take a closer look at some other statements Christ made regarding the will of God.

> *I seek to do not my own will but the will of him who sent me. John 5:30*

"Lo ger boaeno sbyon, elo sbyonoh d man d shdran" (Syriac Aramaic)

We know who sent Christ into the world. It was His Father, But Christ and the Father are one and the same:

> *Philip said to him, "Lord, show us the Father, and it is enough for us." Jesus said to him, "Have I been with you so long, and you still do not know me, Philip? Whoever has seen me has seen the Father. How can you say, 'Show us the Father'? Do you not believe that I am in the Father and the Father is in me? The words that I say to you I do not speak on my own authority, but the Father who dwells in me does his works. Believe me that I am in the Father and the Father is in me, or else believe on account of the works themselves. John 14:8-12*

It is clear from the above quotes that Christ came to do the work of the one who sent him. Since the one who sent Him dwells within Him and both are one and the same, Christ came to do His own work. This work is not directed by the ego, however. It is the expression of His Higher Self, the Divine within, His Christ Consciousness. Christ came to show us the way and since He is the way, it behooves us to follow His example. We, too, are here to do the will of the divine residing within us. This is the will of our Higher Self.

What exactly are we supposed to do with our lives? *"Will"* is a translation of the Syriac Aramaic, "sbyonoh." Sbyonoh means, not only will, but also desire, wish and *pleasure*. If we substitute pleasure for will, our purpose in life becomes clear.

> *"Fear not, little flock, for it is your Father's good pleasure to give you the kingdom. Luke 12:32*

We are here to establish the Kingdom of Heaven on earth starting with our lives.

If Christ came to do, not His will, but the will of Him who sent Him, does this mean that Christ had no will of His own?

Christ is the prototype, the example we need to follow. Just like us, He had two wills; the will of His lower self, the ego and the will of His Higher Self which is the same as the will of His Father, God. Metaphorically speaking, the will of the ego is that of the Devil, while the will of the Higher Self is that of God.

This is our story; we can do the will of our ego or the Devil, or we can do the will of our Higher Self or God.

A simple example, *"Thy will be done on earth as it is in heaven."*
"Nhweh sbyonokh aykano d bashmayo oph b aroh."

Example

This is an extremely basic example, yet it illustrates what

"the will in heaven" and *"the will on earth"* are in our daily lives.

A few days ago, I got the urge to watch a movie that I had seen a long time ago, *"Arn."* I had the option of ignoring the feeling or giving in and watching the movie. I decided to watch the movie with my wife who also enjoys this movie.

When Arn's mother got blood poisoning in the movie, I heard the statement, *"it is the will of God".* I also heard several references regarding Arn, such as: "God has a plan for you." Right away, I began to reflect on these statements because I was in the process of writing this book and the topic I was on was, *"thy will be done on earth as it is in heaven."* Instantly, I began getting ideas as to how I can explain this. I paused the movie, got up and began writing down the ideas that came to me. These ideas developed and became incorporated here as an essential element of this chapter.

Where did the idea or the urge to watch an old movie come from? How did that idea develop to be part of this book?

"Urges" or "ideas" we receive, are *"the will of God in heaven."* Acting on the urges, writing down the ideas and incorporating them in this book, are *"thy will be done on earth as it is in heaven."* Since writing and teaching are an essential aspect of my mission in life which is "Enlightenment and Peace on Earth", I am easily inspired as to what I should do next. Once I acted on the urge and wrote down the ideas, I felt content and was happy.

Contrary to what people may believe, the purpose of life

is **NOT** "the pursuit of happiness." It is to grow in our understanding, to learn and to fulfill our mission in life which is the reason why we were born. *Expressing the will of our Higher Self is what gives us happiness.*

Questions to consider:

1. Are we here due to accident and pure chance?
2. Have we been sent here? Or,
3. Are we here of our own accord?

If we are here by accident and pure chance, we will only seek pleasure and self-gratification. We will not pray, worship or have an inner urge to seek a meaning to our lives.

If we have been sent here by anyone other than ourselves, then that robs us of our freedom of choice.

Since I believe that we have free will, my only option is to believe that we are here of our own accord. It is the *pleasure* of our Higher Self to have us be here to have life and to have it abundantly. We do this by seeking treasures that do not spoil and by living to fulfil our mission.

Because we have free will, we must choose between two wills, the one of the ego and the other of our Higher Self. Choosing the way of the ego, we become the Prodigal Son. Choosing the way of our Higher Self, we become Christlike. Becoming like the Prodigal Son, we lose our way. Becoming Christlike, we stay on course. There are many more ways we can lose our way and become lost, than stay on course:

1. If we pursue our selfish desires and lust for our perceived wants, then we are doing our will, the

will of our ego rather than the will of our Higher Self;

2. If we live in fear, express anger, jealousy, hatred and the other lower emotions, we are giving our ego a free hand. If we are motivated by revenge, violently abusing others, then we are doing the will of the ego. If we use our will to subjugate, coerce and bully others for our own advantage, we are certainly doing our will, the will of the ego and not the will of our Higher Self;

3. If we use our privileges to further our own interests at the expense of others and without regard to the welfare of anyone other than ourselves, then we are expressing our will, the will of the ego and not the will of our Higher Self;

4. If we believe that we are better than others, then it is our ego that is in charge and not our Higher Self;

5. If we cannot express love, care, compassion and concern for others, then our ego is running our life and not the Higher Self.

The simplest way to do the will of our Higher Self, the will of God, the Father, and the will of the one who sent us, is to:

1. Connect to divinity through meditation, prayer and attunement to receive the intuitive impulse or guidance to know what to do next;

2. Once we "hear the Voice Within", we must follow

it and just do it;

3. We must inquire as to what our purpose in life is. We must find out what we are expected to do. We must be open to inspiration. Once we know what our next step is, we proceed. We never wait to see the entire picture, just the next step we need to take;

4. We must trust and rest assured that Listening to the Voice Within is the most effective way to live;

5. We must never resist, but must allow the will of God to function through us.

It is easy to be distracted and get lost. Yet, we *can* stay on course. We have three indicators that point the way for us. These reveal the reason for our birth and the purpose of our lives. The three pillars pointing the way for us are our:

1. Passion;
2. Circumstances; and
3. Synchronicities.

Following our passion, examining and making full use of our circumstances and taking full advantage of our synchronicities will place us on the accelerated path to live and manifest our destiny, the purpose for which we are born.

AMRA

AMRA is a spiritual law of compensation. It states that if we receive, we must give back in turn. And if we want to receive, we must first give. We should live by complying with the law of AMRA. In other words, if we have been blessed, then we are obligated to return the favor and bless the lives of others. We are not here just for ourselves but for others as well. We also need to develop and to mature and we need to help others do likewise. Our *general* goals are to:

1. Regulate our thinking, feeling and desires;
2. Fine tune our talents and abilities;
3. Acquire new skills and continuously cultivate our minds;
4. Master interpersonal relations and learn to direct the energies of our bodies, emotions, mind and creativity toward productive venues that benefit us and others.

Our *specific* goal is to master one or more of our life-lessons. According to Kryon (Lee Carroll), these are:

1. Learn to love;
2. Learn to listen;
3. Learn to receive;
4. Learn to love yourself;
5. Learn to speak your truth;
6. Learn not to be a victim;
7. Learn not to let anyone define you;
8. Learn how to feel your own mastery;
9. Learn how to live with others;
10. Learn how to get out of blaming others;
11. Learn how to drop your karma;
12. Learn how to take care of yourself more than others;

13. Learn that you deserve to be here and that you are not dirty when you are born.

I would like to add:

14. Learn to empower others without creating dependencies.

It is easy to find out what our specific life-lessons are by examining our circumstances. Mine are to master forgiveness, patience and to eliminate buried anger from my childhood. To master a life-lesson, we must face adversity. This is a key factor that we need to understand and accept. We cannot grow unless we are challenged, placed in stressful situations and tested to our limit.

Accepting "No" as an answer

By stating, "***Thy Will Be Done on Earth as it is in Heaven***", "*nhweh sbyonokh aykano d bashmayo oph b aro*", we are indicating that we will allow the will of our Higher Self to manifest through us regardless of what it is, even when the answer is negative, a no.

There are numerous instances in my life where things did not go my way. I "failed" on several occasions. Yet, these failures were exactly what I needed. Our Higher Self knows what is best for us. While we are focused on the here and now, our Higher Self clearly sees our entire future.

1. I was about to graduate with honors from basic training. My Higher Self had other plans. Due

to a weapon's test failure, I did not graduate or receive my promotion. Yet, because of my failure, I ended up at Ft. Meade, Md instead of going to Ft. Sam Houston in Texas. This failure made all the difference in the quality of my life.

2. I also failed a lab test in college without which I would have never immigrated to the United States.

3. If I had succeeded in my first love, I would have never met my wife.

4. I was passed over for promotions on numerous occasions because of politics. This was a signal for me that this career was not for me.

Failures are as important as succusses. Failures correct our course and place us on the right path to reach and manifest our destiny.

In summary

"Thy will be done on earth as it is in heaven"* can be simplified as, *"Thy will be done through me." A prayer:

Dear Higher Self:

1. I recognize that I am here of my own free will;

2. I am here because of a plan and a purpose that I chose;

3. However, I do not remember this plan or

purpose that I decided upon while I was in the spirit world. As soon as I was born, I began to forget my purpose. I was focused on the here and now. There are many distractions along my way. Give me the wisdom to use my free will and make the right choices;

4. *I want to make sure that whatever it was that I wanted to do while I was in spirit world,* **is exactly what I do now that I am on Earth;**

5. May I live on Earth as you, my Higher Self, intended for me to live;

6. **Thy will**, my Higher Self be done, not mine, the ego self.

A puzzle demystified

Have you ever wondered why certain things in your life were so easy to do while others were so hard to carry out? Why certain things come our way easily while others run away from us? Why do we succeed at some and fail at others?

This has happened to me on several occasions. Certain events took place effortlessly while others did not happen even with a great deal of effort. I have experienced miracles in my life. Things that could not happen and should not have happened, yet they did; and conversely, simple things that should have happened, but did not. Why?

The answer lies in the Lord's Prayer and the current topic

of our discussion:

*"**Thy Will Be Done on Earth as it is in Heaven.**" "**Nehwe sbyonokh aykano d bashmayo oph b aro.**"*

Events aligned with our life's purpose unfold effortlessly. Distractions, on the other hand, fortunately, do not manifest. Many refer to this as: It was meant to be or it was not meant to be.

While in the spirit world, we decided on what we needed to do once we were born. We sketched the map and placed signposts in various locations and we gave ourselves reminders at major intersections. We planned out what we wanted to do and experience. If we follow the plan, everything seems to work out fine and Heaven and Earth are glad to do our bidding and help us achieve our goal. In this case, "God" is with us. We are lucky and things work out for us.

If, on the other hand, we take a detour and forget our main reason for being here and pursue distractions instead, things might or might not work out for us. In this case, we are on our own. This is why, for example, we cannot visualize or pray for promotions we do not deserve. Getting a job we are not qualified for might not be in our best interest. We must deserve and qualify for what we seek. If we selfishly ask for things at the expense of another, we are doing the will of our ego instead of the will of our Higher Self. Unless what we ask for is part of the plan for our life, it is best that we fail. Otherwise, if we get what we selfishly ask for, it could ruin our life. Ultimately, we only want to succeed at doing our Father's will, for that alone gives us contentment and satisfaction.

Our attitude should be:

I will always do my best in all that I participate in;
I will have no attachment to the outcome;
My prayer is always: "Thy will be done, not mine."

❖ ❖ ❖

The Higher Self works in mysterious ways
A demonstration

As my separation from the Army at Ft. Meade, MD, neared, I began counting the days until I was a civilian once more. I was oblivious to what the future held for me and I gave it no thought. My only focus was counting the days until my discharge.

I had no plans for my life after discharge. I had nowhere to go. I had no parents or a home to go to. My sister was in college; my two brothers were married with their own families and my youngest brother was in the Navy. The only state I could go back to was Massachusetts, but that is where I could not find a job and was the reason I joined the Army in the first place.

I was to be discharged on July 31, 1975.

In February 1973, I joined the Rosicrucian Order and began my spiritual studies in earnest. As soon as I learned about the Higher Self as an aspect of God within me, I made a solemn compact with this Higher Self. I clearly, resolutely and with conviction stated that: "Not my will be done, but Thine." Additionally:

    1. I never, ever want to take advantage of anybody;

2. I do not want to succeed at the expense of a more deserving person;
3. I want to be an agent of light, dispelling darkness wherever I find it;
4. I want to discover and live my mission in life;
5. Most importantly, if I ever undertake a selfish act, I want to fail at it. I only seek my Higher Self's guidance in matters that further the purpose and mission of my life;
6. Finally, I place my life and my future in your hands. Just show me the way and I will step forward and act fearlessly.

When I first came to Ft. Meade, MD in October 1972, I was placed in the Veterinary Medicine Section under a Captain who was in charge. Even though the work was easy and I was good at it, something within me urged me to switch to Electron Microscopy. I never understood or questioned the urge. It was not easy getting to work in Electron Microscopy. They did not need anyone new there and I did not have the experience. I asked for a transfer. I was refused. I persisted. I pleaded with my boss and talked with the Lieutenant in charge of Electron Microscopy, repeatedly asking for a transfer. Eventually, after several weeks of pleading, they relented and I was transferred to work with the Lieutenant, my new boss in Electron Microscopy.

A year or so later, my new boss received a promotion and was accepted to go to Medical School. He left me in charge. Electron Microscopy requires skill and specialized knowledge of cytology and running a highly complicated microscope. It was a highly skilled position. I was the only one in the section doing Electron Microscopy.

A few weeks before my discharge, the Commanding Officer of the laboratory saw me in the hallway and asked me what I was going to do after my discharge. I told him frankly that I had not given it any thought and I had no idea what I would do once I left. He then asked me if I would like to keep my job as a civilian. I said, sure.

This was the simplest transfer imaginable. The paperwork was taken care of and I was hired as a civil servant. I was discharged on July 31, 1975 and began my civil service at the same job on August 1, 1975. Had I not been offered the job at Ft. Meade, I would have had to return to Massachusetts. I would have struggled and my life would have been unbearable.

It was my Higher Self who came to my rescue. The urge to switch to Electron Microscopy was not a random whim. I was offered the job because there was no replacement for me for the work to continue. The person doing the work had to be specially trained and skilled enough to carry on the specialized work. I did not realize how fortunate I was until years later. My Higher Self came to my rescue once more. Because I had dedicated myself to carry out my life's mission, I was shown the way. As is often the case, we do not realize the significance of an experience until years later.

If our motto is "*thy will be done*" and accept the results regardless of what they are, then things work out for us and we stay on course. What does not work out is often an unnecessary distraction that will veer us off our path. Getting off course is not bad. It just takes too long to reach a destination.

GIVE US THIS DAY OUR DAILY BREAD

God gives us the ingredients for our daily bread, but he expects us to do the baking! — Chip Ingram

The teachings of Christ are not a continuation of the teachings of the Old Testament. The old teachings are based on law. The teachings of Christ are based on grace. This is obvious when we take a closer look at His teachings, especially the Sermon on the Mount and the hidden meanings in the parables. Christ, by teaching us to "ask for our daily bread" instead of laboring for it is moving us from being under the law to living in grace.

> *And to Adam he said,*
>
> "Because you have listened to the voice of your wife and have eaten of the tree of which I commanded you, You shall not eat of it,' cursed is the ground because of you; in pain you shall eat of it all the days of your life; thorns and thistles it shall bring forth for you; and you shall

eat the plants of the field. By the sweat of your face you shall eat bread, till you return to the ground, for out of it you were taken; for you are dust, and to dust you shall return." Gen 3:17-19

Asking for our daily bread is not the same as **"in pain you shall eat all the days of your life."**

Cursed is the ground because of you; in pain you shall eat of it all the days of your life; thorns and thistles it shall bring forth for you; and you shall eat the plants of the field.

How horrible! What a terrible curse!

Once more, we will look at the four levels of interpreting this statement: **"Give us this day our daily bread." "Hablan lahmo d soonkonan yaomono," Syriac Aramaic.**

The simple interpretation

We are reminding ourselves that we must ask God for our necessities because God is the source of all that we need. We should not be greedy, asking only for the most basic bread for sustenance.

When I was young living with my parents in poverty, hearing the Lord's Prayer recited, I wondered why are we asking only for bread when we can ask for a sumptuous meal? After all, isn't God the source of everything? Then I thought that perhaps we should learn not to be greedy and be satisfied with the necessities of life.

Obviously, asking God for our necessities contradicts the

fact that we must work for our livelihood and must earn our keep. So why is Christ teaching us to ask God for our daily bread? There must be more to this statement.

The symbolic interpretation

The assumption is that the bread we are asking for is not simply bread, rather it stands for our needs. The asking is a mere reminder that the ultimate source of all that we have is God. Accordingly, everything is a gift from God.

The spiritual interpretation

The bread we are asking for is **nourishment**. Since we are more than the physical body, the nourishment we are asking for is for our entire being, the physical, the astral and the spiritual bodies. To fully realize the significance of this statement, we must look into the personal interpretation.

The personal interpretation

"Give us this day our daily bread." "Hablan lahmo d soonkonan yaomono," Syriac Aramaic.

Christ makes it clear as to what the bread is:

> *Jesus said to them, "I am the bread of life. Whoever comes to me will never be hungry, and whoever believes in me will never be thirsty. John 6:35*

If Christ is the bread of life, then what we are asking for is a bit of Christ. But what exactly are we asking for?

We are asking for light! This is so because Christ says that is what He is:

> *Again Jesus spoke to them, saying, "I am the light of the world. Whoever follows me will never walk in darkness but will have the light of life." John 8:12*

But, what is the light of life?

Light is wisdom and understanding. It is knowledge of the spiritual laws and the secret teachings of Christ. If life is living and experiencing, then the wisdom we gain through life's experiences, is the light that is Christ, the bread of life that sustains us.

Life is meant to be lived. As we live, we are to learn and to progress in our understanding and we are to gain in wisdom. Life is not meant to be easy. Easy does not help us grow and mature. This is why, as we live, we face challenges. These can become either obstacles that block our progress or they can be stepping stones if we overcome them and gain mastery.

The experiences of life are the **bread** that we are asking for. These experiences are the **nourishment** that we need to sustain our growth. These experiences must be **"chewed"** to extract their hidden value. The piece of Christ we are asking for, is food on all levels. The most important of which is the spiritual nourishment. It is Christ's spiritual teachings that nourish and sustain us.

In Matthew, it is stated:

> *The tempter came and said to him, "If you are the Son of God, command these stones to become loaves of bread." But he answered, "It is written, 'One does not live by bread alone, but by every*

word that comes from the mouth of God." Matt 4:3-4

In other words, we are more than a physical body. We have a spiritual body that requires sustenance as well. While physical bread nurtures the physical body, the Word of God, the spiritual teachings of Christ, and our experiences, nurture and nourish our soul. The physical body dies and with it all the bread that we have ever eaten. But the spiritual body is eternal and the food we give it in the form of the light of Christ— spiritual knowledge, wisdom and understanding, are cumulative and eternal. These never die. That is why it is stated:

> *I am the bread of life. Your ancestors ate the manna in the wilderness, and they died. This is the bread that comes down from heaven, so that one may eat of it and not die. I am the living bread that came down from heaven. Whoever eats of this bread will live forever; and the bread that I will give for the life of the world is my flesh. John 6:48-51*

Light, life, wisdom and understanding are the body of Christ and the "bread" from heaven. He who eats them will never die in the spiritual sense because these are food for the "soul."

*Christ was born in **Bethlehem**.*

> *Now after Jesus was born in Bethlehem of Judea in the days of Herod the king, behold, wise men from the east came to Jerusalem, Matt 2:1*

Bethlehem in Syriac Aramaic means, "**the house of bread.**" "**Beth**" meaning house and "**lehem**", meaning bread. If

Bethlehem is the birthplace of Christ, or the house that produced the bread that is Christ, then Christ as spiritual bread is the bread of life and *the spiritual manna from heaven.*

That is also why Christ gave his "body" to eat during the Last Supper. His "body" is the spiritual teachings He promulgated. (For a detailed explanation of the significance of the Last Supper, please refer to my book: **The Secret Teachings of Christ**, *based on the parables*).

"Eating His body" is the way to eternal life. This is not cannibalism. For to eat, in the spiritual sense, is to consume and to assimilate. Once spiritual lessons are assimilated into us, our epi-soul grows until eventually we attain conscious immortality. Once the teachings of Christ are "eaten", we will gain the light of wisdom and understanding. This light will gradually erode the veil blocking our view so we can see clearly, hear unambiguously, know who we are and live accordingly.

Eating the body of Christ is analogous to eating from the Tree of knowledge—a source of light, wisdom, and understanding. It is having an enlightening experience. It is an AHA moment, a revelation, The veil lifts, our eyes open and we "know good from evil." This is exactly what happened to Adam and Eve when they ate of the fruit of the tree of Knowledge. Their eyes opened and they realized that they were naked and hid themselves. They were "***naked***" because they had no spiritual knowledge.

Our Daily Bread

"Give us this day our <u>daily</u> bread." "Hab lan lahmo d

soonkonan yaomono."

We are not asking for a large amount of **"*bread*",** rather, what is sufficient for today—only what we can consume and manage at this time. This is significant because, just as the size of our stomach is limited, our ability to bear difficulties and tolerate pain and suffering are limited as well. Our trials and tribulations can be overwhelming and the "bread" that we need to learn, to grow and to mature from can lead to our demise. In other words, the amount of "bread"—difficulties and challenges—we are asking for, the piece of the body of Christ we are seeking, must be the right amount for our current needs or what we can handle. It is based on our circumstance and the level of our understanding. We are asking for experiences that confer light upon us but this light needs to be just the right amount so we can "digest" it and handle our current situation. If we get too much "bread" or difficulties that we cannot deal with, we could get indigestion and become ill. In other words, we could break down.

By saying: **"*give us*"**, we are acknowledging that the Father, or God, whom we are asking is the source of our nurturing, nourishment, and experiences. Let us repeat that. **By asking God the Father for our daily bread, we are acknowledging that He is the source of all of our experiences, including the difficult and challenging ones.** In other words, we are admitting that we need the painful experiences as well as the pleasant ones in order to grow and mature. Hence, all that we receive in the form of spiritual "bread", or experiences, are from the Father because *we are asking for them*.

Our experiences are gifts from the Father. Can you imagine how our lives would change if we only understood this? That all of our experiences are gifts from God? In other words, we must go through the experiences and glean whatever we can from them. These are the precious nutrients necessary for our spiritual growth. It is useless to complain about our experiences, for our experiences are meted to us based on what *we need* to grow and mature at every stage of our lives. These experiences are the light that is Christ. They will gradually transform us from a "Child of Man" to a "Child of God." Manifesting our individuality as **a Child of God** is our ultimate destiny and heritage.

We must keep in mind, though, that as we receive the light and become wiser, it is our responsibility in turn, to help those in need. This is according to the spiritual law of AMRA. As we receive, so must we give back; and the more we give, the more we receive in turn. We do not live for ourselves alone. We live to improve ourselves and help elevate humankind.

An Exercise

Imagine that you are invited to a feast or banquet. As you walk into the house and enter the dining room, you see a long table in the middle of the room. On this table is a basket with only one piece of bread. As you approach this table, all your parts, your physical, emotional, mental and spiritual bodies are hungry and starved for nourishment.

You approach the table and the basket. You look at the

bread and hesitate:

"Should I eat this bread or should I leave it alone?" You are not sure. This is not what you were expecting when you responded to the invitation. Yet your hunger for nourishment overwhelms you. You reach and grab that single piece of bread. It is all you have for now. As you touch the bread, you notice that it feels different. It is not an ordinary piece of bread. With reverence, you put the piece of bread into your mouth and consume it. Instantly the bread transforms itself into Light, the true body of Christ—instant transubstantiation!

Instantly, your entire being is nourished. Your body, emotions, mind, and spirit are all nurtured, and you are satiated. You feel and know that you are a being of light and love. You are a child of God, a being with divine heritage. Your eyes open. You see clearly and you understand.

Each of our worldly experiences is a piece of the body of Christ. When we pray using the Lord's prayer, we are asking for our experiences. They are not heaped on us. ***They are the answers to our prayers.*** Some of what we receive is not what we want. It is, however, what we need. We might not desire hardships, difficulties, and challenges, but they are what we need at this time for our growth.

We might not like to see others go hungry, be naked, or suffer from disease. It might be what we need to see at this juncture of our lives because there might be something we can do to help the situation.

We might not want to live in a world engulfed in wars where the unscrupulous take advantage of the weak, and where the criminals prosper. It might be what we need to experience to realize that reality is what we create and that we are never meant to be idle bystanders. If we want our world to be better, we must do our part. We must first work on ourselves and then contribute to the changes we seek.

The world is what it is. What matters is how we view ourselves and the role we play to bring about the changes that we desire. The question we should be asking ourselves is, "What am I doing to create the world as I want it to be.?" Consider the dramatic example of the life of Christ.

The Passion of Christ

The Passion of Christ, a movie by Mel Gibson, had a dramatic impact on its viewers. This movie also generated many controversies.

- Is so much violence in the movie necessary and appropriate?
- Is the movie anti-Semitic?
- Is the movie authentic?
- Who killed Christ?

Who killed Christ? **We** did through our stupidity and ignorance. Did Christ come to die for our sins? Nonsense. We killed Him and then we justified our action by stating that it was His mission to die for our sins.

A movie is a movie. It is not reality. It does not have to depict events as they actually took place for no one knows exactly what happened. It was a great movie. The acting was superb and the use of Aramaic, the common language of the era, was impressive to say the least. However, watching a movie that is very well done does not make it historically correct or a reflection of what really took place. It is only an expression of the viewpoint of a person or a group of people.

At first glance it appears that all the parts of the story fit together well and there is seamless transition from one event to the next. Upon closer examination, however, it is easy to see that the narrators picked and chose from the gospels what they wanted us to see.

The 4 gospels do not agree on what happened to Jesus. They differ in their narratives. There are different versions of the crucifixion and what supposedly took place in the life of Jesus. If we compare the various gospels, the differences become obvious. For example:

- Was there one thief, 2 thieves or no thieves who were crucified with Jesus?
- Were they both ridiculing Christ or only one who did?

What was missing from the movie was the most important aspect of Christianity—***the message of Christ***. What was His message?

What was the meaning of the life of Christ? What was Christ trying to tell us through His life, passion, death and resurrection?

The spiritual meaning of the passion of Christ is one of the most practical aspects of Christianity and it has to do with the topics of this book. Specifically,

"Give us this day our daily bread" and **"Thy will be done on earth as it is in heaven."**

The message of Christ is that *He is the example of what we can be.* Christ is someone we must emulate. His story is our story. He represents humanity. *We gave Him all He can handle. We pushed Him to the limit and He did not cave in. We mocked and humiliated Him and He did not respond in kind. We speared and crucified Him. He forgave us for we know not what we are doing.*

Christ is the seed that grew up and reflected its nature and source—Divinity. He came from God and to the Father He returned. He wanted to show us, not only who He was, but also who we are.

> If He was the Son of God, we are the children of God.
> If He was light, we have the light of God within us.
> If He was life, we have the potential for the abundant life.
> If He was the resurrection, we can resurrect ourselves from being spiritually dead to eternal life.
> If He did not die, we do not die.
> If He ascended to heaven, we can ascend to heaven in our consciousness, but only if we open our eyes and get to *Know Ourselves*, *Love Ourselves* and *Express Ourselves* as children of God.

The life of Christ is a great demonstration of how we can and should live. What the suffering of Christ tells us is that He had the ability and the power to *transcend*. He had a choice. He could summon a legion of angels and show the pathetic humans who the Lord is and who really has power. Instead, He took this opportunity to demonstrate how we should behave. There is no more *"an eye for an eye"*; instead, *forgiveness,* "for they know not what they do."

The mission of Christ and His message are clear:

> *Treat me anyway you want to. I choose how I respond. I will not respond in kind. If you treat me badly, I do not have to do the same. Instead, I will bless you and wish you well. This is my experience and I choose what to make of it.*

To paraphrase St. Francis of Assisi:

> *I will sow love where there is hatred;*
> *And pardon where there is injury;*
> *Faith where there is doubt;*
> *Hope where there is despair;*
> *And light where there is darkness.*

Christ is Light, Life and Love. He acted in a manner that is consistent with His nature. From His actions, we can clearly see that Christ has attained the Kingdom of Heaven. If we want to attain the Kingdom of God ourselves and demonstrate it in our lives, we can emulate Christ and act with compassion, love, and understanding. We can shun violence and not respond to evil with evil. **The era of *"an eye for an eye"* is over.**

This is our world. We help create, mold, and shape it by the way we act or react. We have a choice but only if we learn to use it with discernment. What the world dishes out to us is what is implied in:

Give us this day our daily bread

We are asking for it!

The pain and suffering we encounter are the piece of bread, a slice of the body of Christ that we are asking for. So are our blessings. To make the most of them, we need to recognize them for what they are— spiritual nourishment.

This is the secret of the Eucharist. The bread and the wine will not become the body and the blood of Christ unless we recognize them for what they are. Once we accept our experiences as gifts from the Father, they transform from obstacles into opportunities, from hardships into blessings.

Our choice is how we respond to our experiences:

1. We could react in kind. For example, if someone praises us, we become happy and we praise them in return. If someone criticizes us, we criticize them in return, maybe many times over and in a stronger language. We could complain, quarrel, ridicule, or humiliate our opponents;

2. We could also choose to stop, think, evaluate and act based on what is in the best interest of everyone involved. We can act with love, compassion, understanding and forgiveness as Christ did. We have a choice.

FORGIVE US OUR DEBTS, AS WE FORGIVE OUR DEBTORS

When you forgive, you in no way change the past - but you sure do change the future. — Bernard Meltzer

A court scene in the movie "The Forgiven" has a South African mother facing the man responsible for the brutal murder of her daughter. After pouring out her heart as to what the loss of her daughter meant to her and her family, looking in the eyes of the perpetrator, she said (paraphrased): "I forgive you. We suffered long enough. I need to move forward."

Holding on to grievances keeps us in a whirlwind of negative emotions. It robs us of peace of mind, sleep and negatively impacts our health. It also robs us of a brighter future. That is why Christ taught us to forgive.

There are two different words used regarding

forgiveness in 2 different versions of the Lord's Prayer. One is in Matthew which uses the word "Debt."

> *And forgive us our debts, as we forgive our debtors. Mat 6:12*

The other is in Luke which uses the word 'sin'.

> *and forgive us our sins, for also we ourselves forgive every one indebted to us. Luke 11:4*

There are two aspects requiring forgiveness, acts of commission and acts of omission. In other words, there are two ways we can "sin". We can sin by doing something we should not do and we can also sin by not doing something that we should do. Thus, the 2 words used are debt and sin. Debt is for acts of omission while sin is for acts of commission. The Syriac Aramaic also uses two different words: "*haobo*" and "*htoyo*".

"Wa shbook lan haobayn (haobo) wahtohayn (htoyo) aykano d oph hnayn shbowqan el hayobayn."

"Haobo" is the active component of sin that includes all acts of ***commission***. These are things that we did that are considered sinful such as envy, jealousy, hatred, aggression, malice, and all other forms of sins committed intentionally or otherwise. The English equivalent for sins of commission is "***trespass***" and thus in our prayers we say, "forgive us our trespasses."

"Htoyo" debt, on the other hand, is the passive component of sin. It includes all acts of ***omission***. These are things that we should have done but did not do such as charity, lending a helping hand and caring for others.

The Lord's Prayer in Syriac Aramaic uses both terms together in one sentence. Asking for forgiveness is for both acts of commission and omission. By asking for forgiveness, we are examining our conscience in the presence of our Father. We are reviewing our lives and evaluating our actions. We are asking for forgiveness for all of our sins of commission and omission by us and against us.

Even though it appears that we are asking **God** for forgiveness and that it is God who does the forgiving, it is not so. For the Lord's Prayer is immediately followed with the following statement:

> *For if you forgive men their trespasses, your heavenly Father will also forgive you: But if you forgive not men their trespasses, neither will your Father forgive your trespasses. Matt 6:14*

In other words, forgiveness is in our hands, not the Father's. If **we** forgive, then we are forgiven. If we do not forgive, then there is no forgiveness for us.

This makes perfect sense since part of God resides within us as our Higher Self. Hence, we are connected to divinity at all times. If the divine within us, the Higher Self forgives, then it is forgiven. In other words, forgiveness cannot be lip service. It has to come from the heart/mind involving our entire being.

This is exactly what Christ did. He forgave sins because He was always allowing the Father within Him to act through Him. If Christ forgave, it is because the Father within did so. Christ got in trouble for doing this because people did not understand where Christ was coming from.

> *Why does this fellow speak in this way? It is blasphemy! Who can forgive sins but God alone?" At once Jesus perceived in his spirit that they were discussing these questions among themselves; and he said to them, "Why do you raise such questions in your hearts? Which is easier, to say to the paralytic, 'Your sins are forgiven,' or to say, 'Stand up and take your mat and walk'? But so that you may know that the Son of Man has authority on earth to forgive sins"—he said to the paralytic— "I say to you, stand up, take your mat and go to your home." And he stood up, and immediately took the mat and went out before all of them; so that they were all amazed and glorified God, saying, "We have never seen anything like this!" Mark 2:7-12*

It is clear that sins and forgiveness are between people. God does not withhold forgiveness. We do. God does not judge. We do. There is no sin against God. God is the passive intermediary between the two parties. If and when we forgive others, our sins are forgiven instantaneously.

The Syriac Aramaic word for **to forgive** is *"shbaq."* This word also means to **release** and **to let go**. So, to forgive is to release, to let go of something that we are holding onto that we do not need to do.

What we hold onto takes residence in our minds, hearts, and consciousness. It uses valuable real estate. As negative energy, it saps our vitality and it impacts our health and well-being. We become burdened carrying heavy loads. We weaken and are susceptible to disease and even premature death.

Guilt is a terrible thing to hold onto. It saps our energy and vitality. It can lead to low self-esteem. It can keep us awake at night. It can torment us. What we need to do is to forgive, to release and to let go.

Sins of omission and sins of commission are always in the past. They are behind us and we should be done with them. To hold onto the past and be tortured by it is folly and unnecessary. It robs us of our future. We can and must let go.

There are seven steps to complete forgiveness:

1. First, we must understand that we are here on earth to learn, to grow and to mature. This requires us to face challenges and those who wrong us are teachers in disguise. They are availing us the opportunity to practice. They are testing us. What if it is our life-lesson to master patience and forgiveness? How are we going to practice unless we have an opportunity to be patient or to forgive? Therefore, we must look at those who wrong us in a fresh perspective. They are the ones providing us the necessary opportunity. We must learn to bless them and let go;

2. We must separate actions from the individuals committing the acts. We can judge an action but not the individual responsible for that action. For each is at a different level of maturity. Everyone is in the school of life to learn. Hopefully, we help each other learn as well;

3. We must evaluate the acts of commission and omission for their deeper significance. Why did they

or didn't they occur? What lessons can we learn from these incidents?

4. We must consider compensation. If we were wronged, we must forgive through compassion and understanding. If we wronged another, we must ask for forgiveness in complete sincerity and we must offer to compensate. Having forgiven others, we must also forgive ourselves;

5. We must resolve to learn from the experience and never let it happen again;

6. We must let go, release, cleanse ourselves and move on;

7. Finally, if we were forgiven, then we are obligated by the law of AMRA to return the favor. Having received, we must find a way to give back. We must become more forgiving, tolerant and understanding of people's shortcomings. We must do something worthwhile for another to demonstrate our gratitude.

To forgive is to accept responsibility for our lives and to let go of our tendency to hold others responsible for our plight in life. When we forgive, we remove the blockages that hinder the movement of our life force. Our energy increases and our ability to live our lives unencumbered is enhanced.

Example

I met a young lady while at Ft. Meade, MD who had warts on her hands and other body parts. I inquired about the warts and what she was doing about them. She would not tell me. After becoming good friends, she confided in me as to the cause underlying her problems. She was hiding a secret from her parents and harboring guilt. She was also under tremendous stress.

I encouraged her to confess, admit her mistakes, forgive herself and have a fresh start. She agreed. After confessing and admitting her wrongdoing, she expressed remorse and asked for forgiveness. This encounter was cathartic. After releasing and letting go, she forgave herself. She felt lighter, "cleaner" and more energetic.

The very next day, miraculously, about 90% of this young lady's warts vanished. Within 2 days, they were all gone. She was 100% cured. This was a demonstration of the power of forgiveness to heal. It was truly a miracle to behold.

Sin

It is unfortunate that some Christian sects emphasize the concept of being born in sin. Sin, if we believe in it, is like a cord that wraps around our neck. It suffocates us. Sin is also a terrible burden to carry. The more sinful we believe we are, the stronger our guilt feelings and the more numerous the cords. It is as if a spider is weaving a cobweb around us. After a while we become immobilized and cease to function effectively. Our self-esteem plummets as a result.

Releasing, letting go and forgiving are the antidotes that unravel our tangled cords and set us free from the spider's web, restoring our vitality. By realizing that we are holding onto the cords and that we are suffocating ourselves, we can let go. We can release and forgive. We can cut the cords and set ourselves free.

We can reject the concept of original sin and do away with it. We can replace it with the more ennobling belief that we are children of God born in love and out of love.

Christ, sin and healing

Christ healed many. Often, all He had to do was to tell people that their sins were forgiven and they would instantly heal. The following is a passage about a paralytic. Matthew and Mark state the story differently:

> *And they came, bringing to him a paralytic carried by four men. And when they could not get near him because of the crowd, they removed the roof above him, and when they had made an opening, they let down the bed on which the paralytic lay. And when Jesus saw their faith, he said to the paralytic, "Son, your sins are forgiven." Now some of the scribes were sitting there, questioning in their hearts, "Why does this man speak like that? He is blaspheming! Who can forgive sins but God alone?" And immediately Jesus, perceiving in his spirit that they thus questioned within themselves, said to them, "Why do you question these things in your hearts? Which is easier, to say to the paralytic, 'Your sins are forgiven,' or to say, 'Rise, take up your bed and walk'? But that you may know that the Son of Man has authority on earth to forgive sins"-he said to the paralytic- "I say to you, rise, pick up your bed, and go home." And he rose and immediately picked up his bed and went out before them all, so that they were all amazed and glorified God, saying, "We never saw anything like this!" Mark 2:3-12*

> *And just then some people were carrying a paralyzed man lying on a bed. When Jesus saw their faith, he said to the paralytic, "Take heart, son; your sins are forgiven." Then some of the scribes said to themselves, "This man is blaspheming." But Jesus, perceiving their thoughts, said, "Why do you think evil in your hearts? For which is easier, to say, 'Your sins are forgiven,' or to say, 'Stand up and walk'? But so that you may know that the Son of Man has authority on earth to forgive sins"—he then said to the paralytic—"Stand up, take your bed and go to your home." And he stood up and went to his home. When the crowds saw it, they were filled with awe, and they glorified God, who had given such authority to human beings. Matt 9:2-8*

The last few words are tremendously important. Let us emphasize their full significance:

> *When the crowds saw it, they were filled with awe, and they glorified God, who had given such authority to __human beings.__*

We, you and me, are the __human beings,__ who are given that authority—the authority to forgive sins. __By forgiving, we heal and are healed.__

A second way Christ healed people, was to tell them that they have been cleaned, or cleansed:

> *And there was a leper who came to him and knelt before him, saying, "Lord, if you choose, you can make me clean." He stretched out his hand and touched him, saying, "I do choose. Be made clean!" Immediately his leprosy was cleansed. Matthew*

8:2-3

Taking this cleansing a step further, we realize the significance of baptism and why it is a *symbolic* act of forgiveness of sins. It does not wash away original sin since no one is born in sin. It symbolically washes, cleanses, and purifies. It makes us whole and holy as a declaration of who we are—pure, sinless and holy children of God. This is exactly what letting go and the forgiveness of sin entails.

While baptism is cleansing by water, life and its experiences cleanse us by the fire of hardships, difficulties and challenges.

A 5-step process to cleanse ourselves of negative imprints

1. Begin by grounding yourself in goodness. Bathe your consciousness with love, beauty and joy. Allow good thoughts and feelings to flood your being.
2. Bring the negative belief (such as low self-esteem) to the forefront of your consciousness. Perhaps, you inherited this belief as a child. Consider the repercussions of this belief on your health and vitality.
3. Resolve not to continue to hold onto this belief. Mentally write it on a piece of paper and then burn the paper. Let go of it. Visualize it floating up into the atmosphere and disappearing from your life.
4. Replace the negative belief with a positive one that ennobles you and raises your self-esteem.

(Such as, you are a child of divinity). Bathe yourself in this new feeling.
5. Repeat this exercise as often as you need to until you are fully cleansed.

Did Christ come to save us from sin?

Many grow up with the belief that Christ's mission was to save us from sin. This is an example of a belief that we can and we must replace with a more positive one such as:

The mission of Christ was to demonstrate what is possible for us humans to be. He was the way, the trend setter. He demonstrated how we can live and treat our "enemies" with love, compassion and understanding.

I remember the first time I was reminded of how sinful I was and that I needed Christ to save me. I was told that I was so sinful that the only one who could save me was the son of God through the shedding of His blood as an atonement for my sins.

This was shocking news. I knew for a fact that I had not committed any sins. It was impossible for me to admit that I was that bad of a person. I could not accept that anyone had to die for sins I never committed. Additionally, I believed that if I commit a sin, then I should be the one who pays for it and not someone else. How could I learn anything from my sins if someone else pays for them? Where is the justice in that? Justice demands that he who commits a sin must compensate for it. I rejected that belief outright. Later, I came to learn that there was a symbolic and spiritual meaning to "being born in sin."

We are born in sin if by sin we mean ignorance and imperfection. None of us is perfect. We are here on earth, to perfect our character and personality. We do this by overcoming our challenges. We have life-lessons that we need to master and we might have a previous **Karmic condition** that we need to compensate for. These are our sins of omission and commission that we need to work out. Hence, we are born imperfect, in "debt" or in "sin."

How Christ saves

> *And she shall bring forth a son, and thou shalt call his name JESUS: for he shall save his people from their sins. Matt 1:21*

Christ came to *"save his people,"* is a translation of the Syriac Aramaic, *"nhawehi l amoh"*. There is a better and a more accurate translation for this statement. It is *"to give his people more life"*. Hence, Christ came, not to save us from our sins, for only we can do that, but rather, He came so we may have life and have it more abundantly.

This is exactly what **"to save"** means. For to save is to preserve a life. If, for example, one prevents another from getting killed, then that person's life is preserved or saved. Saving someone's life or preserving it is to give that person a new lease on life since it would have ended.

Christ saves us by preserving our life and by giving us a new lease on life. This happens when we understand what Christ stands for; better yet, when we know who Christ is. In His own words, He is life. *"I am life."* Hence, the more of Christ we have, the more life we end up with.

Christ is also the *bread of life* or what we learn through

experiencing life. By consuming the bread or life, or by experiencing, we mature and our consciousness rises until we finally attain the Christ Consciousness. Then, we are Christlike, fully alive and are saved. That is what Christ alluded to when he said:

> *Follow me, and let the dead bury their own dead.*
> *Matt 8:22*

We are spiritually dead unless we have Christ's Consciousness within us. The more we let go of the "dead" — "sin", ego, ignorance and evil, the more life we end up with and the more "saved" we become.

A fresh perspective on forgiveness—loving our enemies

We **choose** to be born in a physical body and to the circumstances that we find ourselves in. We become physical because there are "sins" or imperfections we need to work on. There are abilities we want to develop and contributions to make. Therefore, everyone is here for the same reasons— to work out their shortcomings and to also lend a helping hand to others. It is easy to know when we are helping others. It is more difficult to realize when others are helping us, especially when what they are dishing out is not what we want. It is not easy being on the receiving end of unpleasantness. We do not realize that we are receiving a helping hand when someone gives us grief.

More often than we realize, the people who challenge us and push us to our limit are our allies. They are friends in disguise helping us to learn valuable life-lessons. We seldom appreciate the people and the circumstances for who and what they are. How can we ever hate someone who is providing us the opportunity to learn and gain mastery when this is exactly what we need? These individuals provide us with the test we need to demonstrate our ability to rise above our circumstances. We need to learn to take advantage of our challenges and turn them into an opportunity to do good and to excel. We pass our tests when we gain mastery of a situation.

Christ asked us to love our so-called enemies because they are our teachers in disguise. They agreed to assume these roles to help us face our challenges by giving us the opportunity to overcome our shortcomings and eliminate our handicaps. Christ admonished us to love our enemies because our enemies are our friends and family.

> *You have heard that it was said, 'You shall love your neighbor and hate your enemy.' But I say to you, Love your enemies and pray for those who persecute you, so that you may be sons of your Father who is in heaven. For he makes his sun rise on the evil and on the good, and sends rain on the just and on the unjust. For if you love those who love you, what reward do you have? Do not even the tax collectors do the same? And if you greet only your brothers, what more are you doing than others? Do not even the Gentiles do the same? You therefore must be perfect, as your heavenly Father is perfect. Matt 5:43-48*

If we understand this, then there is no need to forgive anyone. We see everyone and each situation for what it is—an aid and an opportunity to improve. Our enemies in this life could be our family members and best friends from a previous life. They agreed to assist us in what we need to learn and master. This does not mean that we have a free pass to go around creating hardships for others. We should never add to anyone's difficulties knowingly. We are actors on the stage of life. We assume different roles to create the necessary circumstances to help each other learn, grow and mature.

LEAD US NOT INTO TEMPTATION

Virtue is nothing without the trial of temptation, for there is no conflict without an enemy, no victory without strife. — Pope Leo I

Stating, "**and lead us not into temptation**," "o lo tehlan el nesyuno," Syriac Aramaic, are we accusing God, the Father of being the one who leads us into temptation? Is God the Tempter, or is it the Devil who tempts us? Could it be that we tempt ourselves? Will the real tempter stand up, please?

Temptation

Temptation is *"the desire to do something, especially something wrong or unwise."* In religion, it is often associated with sin.

> *Woe to the world for temptations to sin! For it is necessary that temptations come, but woe to the one by whom the temptation comes! And if your hand or your foot causes you to sin, cut it off and throw it away. It is better for you to enter life*

> *crippled or lame than with two hands or two feet to be thrown into the eternal fire. And if your eye causes you to sin, tear it out and throw it away. It is better for you to enter life with one eye than with two eyes to be thrown into the hell of fire. Matt 18:7-9*
>
> *Watch and pray that you may not enter into temptation. The spirit indeed is willing, but the flesh is weak." Matt 26:41*

The Bible has several accounts of those who were tested via temptation. Adam and Eve were tempted by the sight of the Tree of Knowledge. King David was tempted by the sight of a beautiful woman bathing. Samson succumbed to seduction by Delilah. Unfortunately, they all gave in to temptation and failed the test. They squandered their opportunity to resist and sublimate their desires.

Temptations are necessary. They are the tests that we must go through in order to demonstrate our proficiency. Temptations are opportunities to showcase our character. Both Christ and Judas were tested. Christ triumphed over the temptations and revealed His true nature—a glorious Son of God. Judas succumbed to temptation and betrayed his master for 30 pieces of silver. Temptation avails us a choice. Like Christ, those who are prepared and are ready do not fear temptations. They welcome them. Those who are not prepared better watch out. Temptations can ruin lives.

To ask the Father to, **"*not lead us into temptation*"** is folly. It will never happen for it defeats the purpose of living, learning and growing. We are here to be tempted and to face our challenges, to overcome them, to grow and to unfold our innate nature.

The temptations that we face are obviously different at each stage of our lives. As children we are tempted by toys and candy. These have minor consequences. As adults, our temptations can have serious consequences. Whatever the case, we are never tested or tempted beyond our capacity to overcome them:

> *No temptation has overtaken you that is not common to man. God is faithful, and he will not let you be tempted beyond your ability, but with the temptation he will also provide the way of escape, that you may be able to endure it. 1Cor 10:13*

Earth is our laboratory, the arena and the stage on which we face our temptations, challenges, and opportunities. What matters is how we behave and what we do in these situations. Hence, instead of asking, *"not to be led into temptation"*; we should ask for the courage and the fortitude to rise above the temptation and to demonstrate mastery of the situation. Our prayer should be: **"God, help me to never, ever take advantage of anyone. Fill me with your grace and courage to not only resist temptation, but to use it as an opportunity to demonstrate mastery."**

Who tempts

1. Others as tempters

> *And he said to his disciples, "Temptations to sin are sure to come, but woe to the one through whom they come! It would be better for him if*

> *a millstone were hung around his neck and he were cast into the sea than that he should cause one of these little ones to sin. Pay attention to yourselves! If your brother sins, rebuke him, and if he repents, forgive him, and if he sins against you seven times in the day, and turns to you seven times, saying, 'I repent,' you must forgive him."*
> Luke 17:1-4

We can lead each other into temptation.

2. God as tempter

The notion that God tempts us comes from the story of Adam and Eve in the Garden of Eden. In this Garden, God planted two beautiful trees and placed them in the midst of the Garden and commanded Adam and Eve not to eat from the fruit of the tree of knowledge lest they die.

> *So when the woman saw that the tree was good for food, and that it was a delight to the eyes, and that the tree was to be desired to make one wise,* [2] *she took of its fruit and ate, and she also gave some to her husband who was with her, and he ate.* [7] *Then the eyes of both were opened, and they knew that they were naked. And they sewed fig leaves together and made themselves loincloths.*
> Gen 3:6-8

Placing a tree in the middle of a Garden and making it "good for food" and "a delight to the eyes", is meant to tempt.

3. The Devil as tempter

We know that the Devil is a tempter because Christ was tempted by the Devil after His 40-day fast in the wilderness.

> *Then Jesus was led up by the Spirit into the wilderness to be tempted by the devil. He fasted forty days and forty nights, and afterwards he was famished. The tempter came and said to him, "If you are the Son of God, command these stones to become loaves of bread." Matt 4:1-3*

Here the Devil is clearly identified as the tempter.

Let us repeat the first verse for emphasize:

> **Then Jesus was led up by the Spirit into the wilderness to be tempted by the devil.**

He was led up by the *spirit* to be tempted by the Devil. Is this the same spirit that had just landed on Him a few verses earlier as a dove that proclaimed *"you are my son you are my beloved in whom I am well pleased"*? Is this the spirit of God leading Jesus into temptation? Is it possible that God does tempt us? Or more accurately, does the spirit of God lead us to the Devil so we may be tempted just as Jesus was?

The temptation of Adam and Eve is one of three famous temptations in the Bible. In their case, the object of the temptation was clearly placed in the center of the Garden and made to look beautiful and desirable. It was obvious that it was God who was tempting Adam and Eve. The story, however, is "veiled" and made to appear that it was the Devil in the form of the Serpent who really tempted Eve to eat of the fruit of the tree of knowing Good from

Evil.

The second temptation story is that of Jesus. Here too we are led to believe that the tempter was the Devil. Upon carefully reading the verses, we note that it was the Spirit of God who led Jesus to the Devil so He would be tested through temptation.

The third temptation story is that of Job. Here, too, Job was tested as a result of a wager between God and the Devil.

> *Now there was a day when the sons of God came to present themselves before the LORD, and Satan also came among them. The LORD said to Satan, "Whence have you come from?" Satan answered the LORD, "From going to and fro on the earth, and from walking up and down on it." The LORD said to Satan, "Have you considered my servant Job? There is none like him on the earth, a blameless and upright man who fears God and turns away from evil." Job 1:6-8*

What is Satan doing in the presence of God? Satan had an open-door policy with God. He could come and go as he pleased to malign human beings before God. Here is a quote from Revelations:

> *Now war arose in heaven; Michael and his angels fighting against the dragon; and the dragon and his angels fought back, but they were defeated, and there was no longer any place for them in heaven. And the great dragon was thrown down, that ancient serpent, who is called the Devil and Satan, the deceiver of the whole world—he was*

> *thrown down to the earth, and his angels were thrown down with him.*
>
> *And I heard a loud voice in heaven, saying, "Now the salvation and the power and the kingdom of our God and the authority of his Christ, have come for the accuser of our brethren has been thrown down, who accuses them day and night before our God. Rev 12:7-10*

Satan, or the Devil, in heaven, in the presence of God, accusing the brethren day and night? How can this be?

Humans have an innate need to make sense of their earthly experiences. We must account for the fact that there is evil in the world. If we assign good to God, then there must be another to take the blame for evil. This other is the Devil, Satan and the Serpent. The duality of good and evil necessitates the creation of a God and a Devil. Since God is good, the Devil must be evil.

We love to take credit for our "good" acts and avoid, like the plague, accepting responsibility for our ignoble actions. To shift the blame away from us, we created the Devil to take the blame. Hence, the tempter—Satan, Serpent or Devil.

> *...For you yourselves know that we are destined for this. For when we were with you, we kept telling you beforehand that we were to suffer affliction, just as it has come to pass, and just as you know. For this reason, when I could bear it no longer, I sent to learn about your faith, for fear that somehow the tempter had tempted you and our labor would be in vain. 1 Thess 3:3-5*

Of course, it was the Devil who makes us do it. Who else? Why accept responsibility for our actions when there is someone else we can blame?

The word Devil is derived from the Greek **"*Diabolos*"**, meaning a traducer, or a slanderer. A traducer is someone who willfully misrepresents facts. Hence Satan is in the presence of God accusing the brethren day and night. That is why, in the Gospel according to John, the Devil is called "father of lies":

> *Why do you not understand what I say? It is because you cannot accept my word. You are from your father the devil, and you choose to do your father's desires. He was a murderer from the beginning and does not stand in the truth, because there is no truth in him. When he lies, he speaks according to his own nature, for he is a liar and the father of lies. John 8:43-44*

The Devil as the father of lies is the source and the progenitor of lies because we do not lie and if we did, it is because we were made to lie by the Devil. The Devil is the personification of all that we attribute to falsehood, confusion, disorder and what we term "evil." If anyone has any of these qualities, they must be from the Devil and the person must be possessed by evil spirits. Yet there is only one source. Goodness and evil are both from the same source. Duality is merely an illusion existing only for comparison. Here is a verse from Isaiah:

> *I form the light, and create darkness;*
> *I make peace, and create evil;*
> *I the LORD do all these things. Isaiah 45:7*

God is the source of good and evil for there is only one source to all that exists. The Bible is full of examples of God's goodness, where he rewards those who please Him. It is also full of his evilness where he severely punishes, or even kills by the thousands, destroying entire towns and cities for acts he judged to be unacceptable. The gods of Good and Evil are mythological products of the human imagination. They have no basis in reality. The only real God is a God of Love, Beauty and Joy.

We are in the image of the gods we create. We are capable of astounding good. Heroes sacrifice their own interests in the service of others. There are those who devote their lives for a worthy cause and make a difference in the lives of many. At the same time, we have those who steal, plunder, abuse, torture, maim and kill. If the good is within us, so is the evil. While the good is our Nobel Self, evil is our selfish ego self. We have met the enemy, (the adversary) and it is us.

As long as we blame others for our actions, we will have a Devil. If the Devil stands for evil, the evil is in us. If the Devil is the personification of falsehood, error, and fallacy, these reside within us. Equally, we are the source of the good, the moral, and the commendable.

Traditionally, we have divided the world into two camps; the spiritual and the material; heaven and earth. While heaven and the spiritual belong to God, earth and the material are relegated to the Devil. To be born on earth is to trap the soul and bind it in matter. It is to be in the domain of the Devil. Freedom from bondage comes when the spirit is released from matter at death. Hence matter and the Devil represent bondage and slavery while spirit and heaven represent freedom. This makes perfect sense as to why the earth is the domain of the Devil and why heaven is the domain of God.

Being in matter and in a physical body is to be exposed to temptations for that is the essence of life. Temptations are meant to lead us into action. Temptations in themselves are neutral. What we do with the temptations and the actions we take reveal our character and the degree of our mastery. Hence, it is folly to ask in our prayer: *"and lead us not into temptation."* We are going to be tempted. There is no escaping it. Perhaps there is another interpretation of this statement. There is.

A different interpretation

> *"And lead us not into temptation."*
> *"o lo tehlan el nesyuno"* Syriac Aramaic

The word *"nesyuno"* has another meaning besides temptation, in Aramaic, the language Christ was using at the time. The root of this word is *"nso"* which like in Arabic, *"nsi"* means to *"forget."*

Additionally, the root word for *"tahlan"* in Aramaic, is *"aal"*, which means to enter. While *"lo"* means *"do not."* Hence *"lo tahlan"* translates as: *"do not allow us to enter."* Adding *"el nesyuno"* gives us: *"And do not allow us to enter into a state of forgetfulness"*, or *may we never forget.*

What we are asking God the Father to help us remember and never forget are the following:

1. We are at all times connected to God, the Father;

2. We have an intimate relationship with God. He resides within us;
3. We are a child of God and so is everyone else;
4. We must not forget that we belong to a spiritual family;
5. We have the power to forgive and when we do, we are instantly forgiven;
6. Having received multiple blessings, we are obligated to give back in service;
7. And most importantly, we must remember and never forget this state of *holiness* established by invoking the name of our Father and by being in His presence.

Essentially, what we are saying is this: "**It is so easy to forget our true nature and become the Prodigal Son. We need to remember who we are at all times and act accordingly.**"

Living in the world is being the Prodigal Son. Often, we find ourselves living like pigs. If we get used to this and accept it as a way of life, we have forgotten who we are. We will not head back home to our Father until one day, through pain and suffering, we are forced to wake up and realize that this is not who we are. Our place is not with the pigs; we can live in a mansion instead.

By succumbing to temptation, we lose our way. Pain, suffering and difficulties eventually help us correct our course. Temptations play a key role in waking us up. By succumbing to temptations, we fall. This, however, does not mean that we are doomed, for we are never judged. We simply face the consequences of our actions. Life will keep presenting us with enough temptations, challenges, and opportunities, until one day we triumph. We wake up and boldly proclain:

> *Give me all the temptations that I can handle this day. For this is my daily bread that will nourish and sustain me.*
>
> *Tempt me and make my day for I now know who I am and nothing will phase me. I know the answers to all the tests and trials. I can pass all challenges with flying colors. I have overcome. The illusion is gone. Maya no more. The veil has lifted. I am awake. I can see clearly, not only who I am, but also who everyone else is and what life is all about. I know why we face difficulties, are tempted, and why we experience pain and suffer. These are our "alarm clock" to wake us up. Once we do, illusions vanish. We were dead then, but no more. We have risen from the tomb.*

DELIVER US FROM EVIL PART I

*Hell is empty and all the devils are here. The world is not threatened by **evil** people, but by those who allow **evil** to take place. — William Shakespeare*

What exactly do we want to be delivered from? Is it evil people? Evil spirits? Or, evil spirits in people? Is there a difference between bad, wrong and evil?

Evil is defined as any act that causes harm, brings sorrow, distress or calamity. There is no denying the existence of evil people in the world. These are the ones who carry out evil acts. Perhaps our world has never been free of evil people. We believe in a duality and a struggle between the two forces of good and evil. Some even believe that in the final days, God and the Devil will have a war and God will win that final conflict and then there will be a Day of Judgment. We consider God to be Good while the Devil is Evil. In many parts of the world the concept of God as

Good does not exist. God is viewed as Unity, as the All and there is nothing else. God is all there is or can be.

The Syriac Aramaic word for God is "*aloho*." In Arabic, it is "*allah*." The word God is derived from the Germanic root, which stands for good. And this creates confusion because the moment we say good, we have to think of evil as well because there is no good without evil. Good and evil go hand in hand. Good seems to be what we want while evil is what we want to be delivered from.

To deliver in the phrase, **"but deliver us from evil", "elo fason men beesho",** means to rescue, to hand over and to set free. We are asking to be rescued from and set free of evil. What exactly is evil? Is it an exaggerated form of bad?

I have a good friend who was in excruciating pain for over a month. The pain was so bad that she had difficulty sleeping at night. She had been seeing all sorts of practitioners except Western doctors. According to her, Western medicine was "bad" because it was invasive while Alternative medicines were "good" because they were natural and holistic. After a lengthy discussion about good and evil, she agreed to see a Western doctor the next day. We need a better understanding of what we mean by good and evil.

The Syriac Aramaic word for good is "*tobo*" while the word for evil is "*beesho*." "*Tobo*" can mean good but it also has several other meanings: *valuable, precious, worth something, cultivated, excellent, honorable, kind, gracious, benevolent, beneficent, favorable and mature.*

"*Beesho*", on the other hand, can mean not only evil

but also: *bad, ugly, error, cruel, mistake, malignant, rotten, unripe, immature, unfortunate, unlucky, wicked, wrong, diseased, incorrect, culprit, deceiver, troublemaker, and the evil one.*

There is a reference in Jeremiah that refers to "***tobo***" (what we call good) and "***beesho***", (what we term evil), in a totally different context that I believe is closer to the original intent. Here is the pertinent passage without the filler information:

> *The Lord showed me two baskets of figs placed before the temple of the Lord. ...One basket had very good figs, like first-ripe figs, but the other basket had very bad figs, so bad that they could not be eaten. And the Lord said to me, "What do you see, Jeremiah?" I said, "Figs, the good figs very good, and the bad figs very bad, so bad that they cannot be eaten." Jeremiah 24:1-3*

Reading this passage from Jeremiah from a different version of the Bible makes the meaning of the words good and bad, very clear:

> *The Lord shewed me, and, behold, two baskets of figs set before the temple of the Lord, ... One basket very good figs, like the figs first ripe: and the other basket very naughty figs, which could not be eaten, they were so bad. Then said the Lord unto me, What seest thou, Jeremiah? And I said, Figs; the good figs, very good; and the evil, very evil, that cannot be eaten, they are so evil. Authorized King James Version (Pure Cambridge Edition).*

From yet another version:

> *And Yahweh said to me: "What do you see, Jeremiah?" and I replied: "Figs, ripe figs, very ripe figs; and unripe figs, very unripe figs, no one can eat them because they are so sour."*

The words used to describe the figs in Syriac Aramaic are *"tobo"* and *"beesho."* While most versions of the Bible translate *"tobo"* as good, and *"beesho"* as bad, a few more appropriately translate *"tobo"* **as ripe** and *"beesho"* **as unripe**. While figs are ripe or unripe, **people are either mature or immature.** The same two Syriac Aramaic words are used to describe people— *"tobo"* **for mature** and *"beesho"* **for immature**. In other words, the "good" situations we face are with mature people while the difficult circumstances we find ourselves in are with immature people.

Here is another example of the use of *"tobo"* and *"beesho"*, good and evil in reference to Christ:

> *I am the good shepherd. The good shepherd lays down his life for the sheep. John 10:11*

When Christ says: *"I am the Good Shepherd"*, what does He mean by a good shepherd? Does one have to lay down his life for his sheep to be a good shepherd?

According to Zecharia Sitchin, author of the Earth chronicles books, Sumerian rulers cherished the title *"en.si"* meaning *"righteous shepherd."* The first king to bear this title was Sargon the first, a common gardener and shepherd selected by the goddess Inanna to be king of Sumer and Akkad. This ruler was righteous, just, and compassionate. He used the law to direct human conduct rather than punish human faults. This king bore the name-epithet *"sharru-kin"*, meaning righteous king. The king was known as the *"righteous shepherd."*

When Christ says, "I am the Good Shepherd", *"enono roayo tobo"*, He is stating that He is a **mature** shepherd of the people. The word used for "good" is *"tobo."* I believe the better translation for *"tobo"*, in this instance, is mature rather than good. This makes more sense than "I am the good shepherd." For, as far as I know, there are no bad shepherds— only mature and immature ones. It is the same with people. There are only mature and immature people.

Good and bad are generic terms and are without much specificity. We should stop using them. Instead, we should be more specific and use descriptive terms. A far better way to make sense of the statement: *"deliver us from evil"*, is to relate it to mature and immature people. Instead of saying "deliver us from evil", we can say "spare us from having to deal with immature people." The immature are almost aways **selfish** and capable of much evil.

Being immature is like having a veil that distorts and obstructs our vision. Immature people are the ones Christ referred to as "having eyes, but they cannot see, having ears, but they cannot hear." Because these people were immature, Christ did not judge them even while they crucified Him.

Being immature is not necessarily being bad or evil even though the acts stemming from immaturity can be. It simply means that immature people are "unripe." They require time to "ripen" and mature. Immature people are not "ready" yet for spirituality and the kingdom of heaven. They need awakening through the cauldron of painful experiences.

This sheds some light on the parable of the ten maidens who were waiting with lamps for the groom. The five maidens who were prepared and ready were termed "good", **"tobo"** or mature maidens while the other five who were not prepared and not ready, were termed "evil", **"beesho"** or immature.

We know how difficult it can be to deal with teens or even with young adults in their twenties. These are some of the most difficult years for relationships. This is because we and our children, frequently are not yet mature enough to have a meaningful relationship.

Dealing with immature people can be some of the most difficult situations we can find ourselves in. It takes skill, patience, commitment, and a sincere desire to hear and understand each other. Only mature individuals have these qualities. Often, we are as immature as those we are dealing with. The situation is a compounded calamity and extremely taxing. The advantage Christ had was that He was mature. He knew how to deal with others who were not. Thus, it was easy for Him to say:

> And Jesus said, "Father, forgive them, for they know not what they do." Luke 23:34

In other words, forgive them Father for they are immature. They are not aware of what they are doing. This was an ongoing occurrence for Christ as He faced immature people throughout His ministry. People were not ready to understand His message and relate to what he was saying. It became so challenging for Christ that He hid His "real" teachings in parables. At one point, He even asked His Father if He could be spared the bitter cup— in other words, to be spared the ordeal of having to teach and interact with immature people.

> *And he went forward a little, and fell on his face, and prayed, saying, My Father, if it be possible, let this cup pass away from me: nevertheless, not as I will, but as thou wilt. Matt 26:39*

Even though Christ asked to be spared the cup, He knew that He must drink of it. He had to go through with His ordeal for that was His mission in life.

So it is with us. We must go through with our experiences, tough as they might be, for they are necessary for our growth, maturation and the completion of our mission.

We might wonder as to why Christ said: "Father, forgive them," instead of saying to the people directly: ***I forgive you for you know not what you do,*** when this is exactly what He is asking us to do in the Lord's Prayer when we say:

> *And forgive us our trespasses as <u>we</u> forgive those who trespass against us.*

For one thing, the people would not have accepted what he had to say. They might have stoned him to death if He had said instead:

> *I forgive you for you do not know what you are doing. You are asleep and you are immature.*

We, too, are immature. We are like **Jeremiah's** figs in one of the baskets. We are green, unripe, and immature. To ripen, mature and become like the good delicious figs, we require a great deal of difficulties, hardships and challenges. It is only through the furnace of pain, suffering and agony that we are exposed to the sun's warming rays and slowly but surely, ripen and mature. Our challenges are the cross upon which our personality unfolds, blossoms and matures.

Where is the evil?

Where is the evil that we are asking to be delivered from? This evil is not out there in the air or in nature. It is in the hearts and minds of people. It is in you and it is in me. We need to be free of it. We need to cleanse our minds of immature "evil" thoughts and purify our hearts with noble feelings towards all.

Instead of asking to be delivered from evil, we need to ask for the courage to face evil and to put an end to it. Better yet, we need to learn how to transform evil into good. What we need is the insight, wisdom and courage to deal with immaturity, selfishness and evil and convert them into opportunities to demonstrate maturity, selflessness and compassion.

Maturity, immaturity, good and evil are a matter of perspective. In time, and sometimes over a long period of time, it becomes apparent that all is good. Even floods, volcanoes and fires eventually produce a great deal of good. They renew, invigorate, and introduce change to our planet.

So it is with us. Eventually, perhaps after a long time,

it becomes evident that all is good and everything is unfolding as it should. Each event and experience is like a piece of a gigantic puzzle. All the pieces are required and must be in place for the picture to reveal itself. Everything is a component of a great plan, an engineering marvel that is the handiwork of the one and only reality—God. Just as we left our childishness behind once we grew up and matured, so will the selfish "evil" people. Over time, they too will grow up, learn and mature. Their eyes will finally open and will see that:

- There is only one body that is Humanity;
- There is only one being that is the Cosmos;
- There is none but the one God that is composite, corporeal, and intangible. You and I, the trees and the animals, the planets and the universes are cells, tissues, organs and systems in this one gigantic body of being. We compose and give flesh to the one and only spirit that is God.

This concept of unity is transformative once we understand its full implications. If there is only unity, then you and I are part of this unity. You and I can never be separated from it or from each other. Together we are one gigantic *family*. Knowing this and living accordingly, our lives become simple and miraculous. It is easy to see how we can be one with our family and friends. It is much more difficult to realize our unity with the ones we do not like, our antagonists and our so-called enemies. Yet, we are all one, in different classes and in diverse roles and guises.

The first person to fully realize the implications of unity was the Pharaoh Akhenaton, who symbolized God with the sun and called this God, Aton. The sun belongs to all living beings and no one can claim possession of the sun by saying that this is my sun. It belongs to everyone. Additionally, the sun is the source of light, warmth and life.

The sun is the source of all material elements as well. This is because the burning hydrogen in the Sun converts to helium through fusion and many of the elements form by successive fusions. The explosion of suns gives rise to the reimaging elements. Hence, the Sun is the source of all light, all matter, and all life. That's why the symbol of God for Akhnaton was the Aton, symbolized by the sun.

Please read the following quote before you do the following exercise.

> *Did you know the average breath you breathe contains about 10 sextillion atoms, a number which, as you may remember, can be written in modern notation as 10^{22}? And, since the entire atmosphere of Earth is voluminous enough to hold about the same number of breaths, each breath turns out, like man himself, to be about midway in size between an atom and the world — mathematically speaking, 10^{22} atoms in each of 10^{22} breaths- multiplying to a total of 10^{44} atoms of air blowing around the planet. This means of course that each time you inhale you are drawing into yourself an average of about one atom from each of the breaths contained in the whole sky. Also every time you exhale you are sending back the same average of an atom to each of these breaths,*

as is every other living person, and this exchange, repeated twenty thousand times a day by some four billion people, has the surprising consequence that each breath you breathe must contain a quadrillion (10^{15}) atoms breathed by the rest of mankind within the past few weeks and more than a million atoms breathed personally sometime by each and any person on Earth. **The Seven Mysteries of Life,** by Guy Murchie.

Exercise

Sit down, close your eyes, relax and take a few deep breaths. Inhale, hold, then slowly exhale. As you breath in, become aware that with each inhalation, *"***you have breathed in more than a million atoms breathed personally sometime by each and every person on Earth.*** Each time you exhale, you are sending out the same number of atoms for others to share. With each breath, you are engaged in an ongoing trade, receiving and giving, nonstop. By breathing, you are cementing your connection with the universe. Everyone is connected with everyone else. There is nothing separate and apart. There is unity, there is only being. You are part of this being, inseparably immersed in it.

Bathe your being in this feeling of unity. Where you are is a center of power because you are connected to the All. Allow the energy of this unity to flood your being. Become aware of a tremendous vitality and power surging through you. You are the mover, the shaper, and the creator. Anything you do in this unity affects all else. What you create here is a blueprint, a seed. Manifestation is only a matter of time.

The moment you touch unity you touch God; you touch your highest aspect of being. The instant you feel your connection to the All, you manifest the Kingdom of Heaven in your life and on your earth.

DELIVER US FROM EVIL PART II
Sex, Sin and Evil

The world is not full of evil because of those who do wrong. It is full of evil because of those who do nothing. — Albert Einstein

The idea of good and evil is introduced in the Bible, in the Garden of Eden, as The Tree of Knowing Good and Evil.

And the LORD God planted a garden in Eden, in the east, and there he put the man whom he had formed. And out of the ground the LORD God made to spring up every tree that is pleasant to the sight and good for food. The tree of life was in the midst of the garden, and the tree of the knowledge of good and evil. Gen 2:8-9

We are admonished not to eat of the fruit of the Tree of Knowing Good and Evil.

The LORD God took the man and put him in the

> *garden of Eden to work it and keep it. And the LORD God commanded the man, saying, "You may surely eat of every tree of the garden, but of the tree of the knowledge of good and evil you shall not eat, for in the day that you eat of it you shall surely die."*
> Gen 2:15-17

How could "eating from a tree" cause us to know good and evil? Why would we die if we knew good and evil? Obviously, eating the fruit of a tree can never cause us to die. There must be more to the story and there is. To know what the fruit of this tree was, we must go to a source much older than the Bible and Genesis—the story of Gilgamesh and Enkidu.

In **The Epic Of Gilgamesh,** there is reference to a man known as Enkidu. Enkidu was conceived as an image, formed of water and clay and was born in the wilderness. This is similar to how Adam was conceived as an image and created from the dust of the ground. There was virtue in Enkidu. *"He was innocent of mankind; he knew nothing of the cultivated land."* "*Enkidu ate grass in the hills with the gazelle and lurked with wild beasts at the water-holes; he had joy of the water with the herds of wild game."* He was a virgin. He had never known a woman. He did not know good from evil.

Enkidu was tempted by a harlot who "taught him the woman's art." Enkidu gave in to the temptation and lost his innocence. Losing his innocence, he gained in worldly knowledge.

> *For six days and seven nights they lay together, for Enkidu had forgotten his home in the hills; but when he was satisfied, he went back to the*

wild beasts. Then, when the gazelle saw him, they bolted away; when the wild creatures saw him they fled. Enkidu would have followed, but his body was bound as though with a cord, his knees gave way when he started to run; his swiftness was gone. And now the wild creatures had all fled away; Enkidu was grown weak, for wisdom was in him, and the thoughts of a man were in his heart. So he returned and sat down at the woman's feet, and listened intently to what she said. 'You are wise, Enkidu, and now you have become like a god. Why do you want to run wild like the beasts in the hills? Come with me." [1]

Adam and Eve ate of the fruit of the Tree of Knowledge of Good and Evil. Their eyes opened and they realized that they were naked. They, too, like Enkidu, became like the gods knowing good and evil. What is more, they did not die as a result of eating from the tree.

For God knows that when you eat of it your eyes will be opened, and you will be like God, knowing good and evil." So when the woman saw that the tree was good for food, and that it was a delight to the eyes, and that the tree was to be desired to make one wise, she took of its fruit and ate; and she also gave some to her husband, and he ate. Then the eyes of both were opened, and they knew that they were naked; and they sewed fig leaves together and made themselves aprons.   Genesis 3:22

Enkidu's eyes opened as a result of the sexual act. He lost his innocence and acquired wisdom becoming like the gods. Adam, also had his eyes open and he, too, became wise. The tree (fruit) Adam was forbidden to eat from was Eve herself. Eve was tempted by a "snake" that was probably the one on Adam located at his center. Adam and Eve lost their innocence as a result of the sexual act. Their eyes were opened and they saw that they were naked. They, too, acquired wisdom and became like the gods. Thus, what appears to distinguish people from the gods is "open eyes" — knowledge and wisdom. To know is to be like the gods. But why is knowing equated with the sexual act?

> ."..Now Adam **knew** his wife, and she conceived and bore Cain.."   Genesis 4:1

> "Then said Mary unto the angel, How shall this be, seeing that I **know** not a man?" Luke 1:34

The ancients referred to the sexual act by calling it **"knowing."** (Adam knew Eve, for example). Modern man refers to the sexual act as "making love." What is the relationship between having sex, loving and knowing?

The state of a person changes dramatically as a result of the first sexual experience. Before the experience, one is innocent, pure, and in a state of **"not knowing."** After the experience, one is transformed into a state of knowing. Having one's eyes closed, not knowing, innocence and sleep is represented by virginity. Wakefulness, gain in worldly knowledge and knowing good and evil (being judgmental) is represented by the loss of virginity. The degree of the transformation depends on the quality of the sexual encounter.

Sex provides us the opportunity to come "face to face" with, join and merge with another in a most intimate and profound way. While in the act of having sex, the two are one. Having sex allows a couple to forget their ego self and get to KNOW each other, intimately, deeply and profoundly. Hence, the death of the individual and the birth of the couple.

What Happens When We Know?

There are two words for "*to know*" in Syriac Aramaic: "*yodaa*" and "*hakem*". "*Yodaa*" is used for the ordinary "to know" as in, "I know your name". The word used in the Bible for when Adam knew Eve, is "*hakem*" which has several meanings: *wise, prudent, intelligent, sensible, learned, skillful, crafty, cunning; a wiseman, sage, magician.* Hence, having sex opens our eyes and transforms us into being wise and all the other qualities.

Knowing gives us a jolt. It awakens us from our slumber. When we know, it is like finding part of ourself that was lost. It is like the Prodigal Son returning home. It is like the question finding its answer. It is like the door opening after we have been knocking for a long time. It is like remembering something that we knew but had forgotten.

Sex, sin and evil

It is obvious from the story of Adam and Eve that the disobedience was not about eating a fruit, it was about not having sex. Why would the God of the Old Testament forbid Adam and Eve to have sex? The aversion to sex is not a command by God, it is the misguided opinion of early influential people. According to Barbara Walker author of, **_The Women's Encyclopedia of Myths and Secrets_**, there are several reasons for the aversion to sex (adapted):

    1. Early believers thought that the Kingdom of God

couldn't be established until the human race was allowed to die out through universal celibacy;
2. The belief in the "saving grace of chastity";
3. Sex is the means of transmitting Adam and Eve's guilt to all generations— the root cause of the Original Sin;
4. Some believed that souls are entrapped in flesh by "the mystery of love and lust";
5. Pagans made sex a central holy sacrament, enacting the union of the Great Goddess and her phallic consort;
6. The early view of Christians was that, "women brought death into the world and sex perpetuated it";
7. The admonition that we should "not love the world neither things that are in the world…the lust of the flesh, the lust of the eyes, and the pride of life, is not of the Father."

Love not the world, neither the things that are in the world. If any man love the world, the love of the Father is not in him. For all that is in the world, the lust of the flesh and the lust of the eyes and the vainglory of life, is not of the Father, but is of the world. And the world passeth away, and the lust thereof: but he that doeth the will of God abideth for ever. 1 John 15-17

It is sad that there was much ignorance in the old days, but it is tragic that it still exists today. This belief ruins lives. I believe in a God who is Love, Beauty and Joy. While lust, abuse and taking advantage of another is evil, love is the epitome of goodness. Loving selflessly, purely, spiritually and wholly is the way to the Kingdom of God and Heaven.

The association of sex with sin has to end. Sex cannot be a sin, unless it is abusive. The role of sex in life is irreplaceable. Without it, none of us would have been born. Who then would glorify God?

If sin is an offense against a religious or moral law, any abuse of a living being is an affront to God. This is because each of us is one of the "hidden" names of God. Hence any evil act against a living being is a sin. We cannot sin against God. God is above our pettiness. We can, however, sin against His representatives, as the living beings on earth. Hence, abusive sex is a sin while sex through love is a sacrament.

Good, bad, and evil

Good is what we like. Bad is what we do not like. Evil is what causes sorrow, distress or suffering and is reprehensible. Good, bad, and evil are relative terms that we use casually. Is nature evil if it brings calamity? Can something as simple as the weather be good or bad?

When the weather is according to our wishes, we term the situation good. Once things go astray and not according to our wishes, we term the situation bad. This happens when it rains too much or does not rain enough; when it is too cold or too hot.

I read the story of an old Sufi who had one son and one horse. One day, the horse took off and disappeared. People came to the Sufi and said to him:
"It is too bad that your horse took off and is gone." The Sufi answered them, "perhaps."

In a few days, the horse returned with a beautiful mare and the people came to the Sufi and told him: "It is so good that your horse returned with a mare." The Sufi answered them, "perhaps."

The next day his son broke his leg while attempting to tame the mare. People came to the Sufi and said to him: "It is too bad that your son broke his leg." The Sufi answered them, "perhaps."

In a few days, soldiers appeared in the village gathering conscripts for the army. They took all the young men but left the Sufi's son alone because of his broken leg. The people once more came to the Sufi and said to him: "How wonderful that your son was not taken with the soldiers." The Sufi answered them, "perhaps."

We measure time by the human yard stick—one life span. A hundred twenty years for us seems like a long time. For flees, bees, ants and microorganisms, a hundred twenty years would be an eternity. In geological time, a hundred twenty years does not even register on the time scale. Our interpretation of what is good, bad, sinful or evil has different meanings viewed from a much broader perspective. Given enough time, the ugly would transform into the beautiful, the bad into the good and sin into grace.

---

[1] The Epic of Gilgamesh, N. K. Sanders, Penguin Books 1972

FOR THINE IS THE KINGDOM, THE POWER AND THE GLORY, FOREVER AND EVER

What is the glory of God? It is who God is. It is the essence of His nature; the weight of His importance; the radiance of His splendor; the demonstration of His power; the atmosphere of His presence. —Rick Warren

Now we come to the last part of the prayer, the cooling down phase. We began our prayer by invoking the presence of our Father, hallowing His name, asking that the Kingdom of God manifest in our lives, becoming aware of our purpose on earth, realizing the value of our experiences as the bread that we need to nourish our various bodies. We also acknowledged the value of temptation and the need to stay connected with our Father. This last part, *"for thine is the kingdom, the power and the glory"* is a doxology or an expression of praise to God. This part was added to the prayer later on and it does not appear in most manuscripts of the Bible. It is only a footnote in the Revised Standard Version. Yet, this part is always used in Syriac Aramaic.

The Lord's Prayer can be divided into 3 parts:

1. A warm up phase where we link to our Father. We do this by invoking the presence of our Father and by hallowing his name;

2. An active phase where we state the purpose of our prayer. We remind ourselves of who we are, why we are here. We ponder the purpose of our lives. We contemplate our circumstances. We highlight the opportunities we have to transform not only our lives, but the lives of others as well. While in this state, we remember our sins of omission and commission. We ask for forgiveness knowing full well that as we forgive others, we are also forgiven. We become fully aware of our role in our lives. We have the power to loosen or bind and, consequently, change outcomes;

3. Finally, we come to the cooling down phase. We acknowledge that on our own we can do nothing. We begin to detach and seal our prayer with the stamp of truth. We bring our prayer to a close and we revert back to our normal state of functioning.

For thine is the kingdom, the power, and the glory. "Metool dilokhi malkutho o haylo o teshbuhto L olam olmin."

This statement is meant to help us do away with our ego. We are too quick to take credit for our successes and achievements. We are eager to claim "the kingdom, the power and the glory" for ourselves. "I did it", we claim. But who among us does not owe their successes to the contributions of others? Who among us did not receive some assistance along the way?

We owe our education to our teachers. We learned our skills building on what others have achieved. Our discoveries, inventions and innovations ride on the shoulders of the giants who preceded us. Without the nurturing of our parents, we would not have survived. Without our country, culture and community, where would we be?

Even though, *in essence,* we are of God and a child of God, in **reality, awareness and behavior**, we are far from it. There is a gulf between our potential as Children of God and our reality as Children of Man. At this stage of our lives, we are the Prodigal son who realizes that he has a family he belongs to and a home he can go back to. We are just beginning our journey back home. **Our knowledge of who we are** is only theoretical at this stage of our lives and is not realized as an actuality or reflected in our behavior.

No earthly being, or even a group of beings, could have planned my life the way it turned out. Imagine the greatest planners on the planet were tasked to plot a path for me to navigate from my starting point to where I am today. Born in Aleppo, Syria to almost illiterate parents, living in abject poverty and speaking a dialect that is a mixture of Armenian, Syriac and Arabic, how would you get me to the United States, happily married with two incredible daughters who are highly successful and with all the experiences I have had? Having lost my mother at a young age, I grew up without a family. I had no birth certificate or any other official documentation such as a passport. Yet, miraculously I graduated from a prestigious university, immigrated to the United States, taught English and life skills for 10 years, and was a Regional Instructor for a worldwide spiritual organization. I also published 6 books in addition to this one. How did I do it? Was it due to my skills, abilities and hard work? Was it due to my "good looks"? Or perhaps it was pure luck.

The answer is none of the above. It was all due to synchronicities orchestrated by my Higher Self. Obviously, I had to do my part. Yet, without the guidance of my Higher Self, the aspect of God within me, in all probability, I would have been dead by now, perhaps killed in one of the Middle Eastern wars.

Therefore, I can honestly and without hesitation state: *"For thine is the kingdom, the power and the glory, forever and ever", "metool dilokhi malkutho o haylo o teshbuhto l olam olmin"*, **because it is true**. I cannot take credit for the way my life turned out. I did my part, but that was merely **Listening to the Voice Within** and acting accordingly. Yet, without the synchronicities, none of these would have been possible.

> *For thine is the kingdom,*
> *the power and the glory,*
> *forever and ever*

> *"metool dilokhi malkutho o*
> *haylo o teshbuhto l olam olmin"*

Let us consider each part separately.

For thine is the kingdom (*metool dilokhi malkutho*)

We are on a journey to manifest the Kingdom of God in our lives. Even though the Kingdom of Heaven is our birthright, we are not mature enough to claim it. Only by acting on the promptings of our Higher Self do we have any chance of attaining our goal. Our progress is slow and gradual.

If we view ourselves as a seed, we must first be planted and establish a root system before we can appear as a seedling. Our life is akin to a structure being built. If we intermittently view a building at various stages of its construction, it is difficult to know what is being constructed until the later phases. So it is with our lives. Once fully grown and mature, we will manifest the Kingdom of Heaven in our lives which is our destiny. Until then, we are merely a bud, a tiny plant, or an infant. We have the potential to manifest the kingdom of God in our lives, but we are far from it. ***But, first, our ego must get out of the way.***

"For thine is the kingdom" might appear contradictory to what Christ stated in the Sermon on the Mount:

> *Blessed are the poor in spirit, for theirs is the kingdom of heaven. Matt 5:3*

Who has the kingdom, God or the poor in spirit? Even though we are saying ***"for thine is the kingdom"***, meaning it is God's, we must not forget that it is ours as well if we **qualify**. The kingdom of Heaven is ours if we are poor in spirit. Being poor in spirit does not mean that we have very little spirit. Far from it. It means that we have put our **ego** aside and have allowed the spirit of God to function through us. In other words, we are allowing the will of God to manifest through us. We are not proud of our accomplishments. We acknowledge that without the guidance of our Higher Self, we are nothing.

For thine is the Power *(metool dilokhi haylo)*

When we state that God has the power, does that mean that we are powerless? Let us take a closer look at the following verses:

> *I can do nothing on my own. As I hear, I judge; and my judgment is just, because I seek to do not my own will but the will of him who sent me. John 5:30*

> *Then Jesus called the twelve together and gave them power and authority over all demons and to cure diseases, and he sent them out to proclaim*

the kingdom of God and to heal. Luke 9:1-2

How can Jesus give power and authority to his disciples when, on His own, He has none and, on His own, can do nothing? This is not a problem once we understand the true nature of power.

Even though there are different forms of power, in reality there is only one power. This power can manifest in different forms just as electricity can manifest variously as it flows through diverse implements. If we hook up to the source of power, then we are plugged into the electric current and we can manifest power. On our own, in other words, independent of being plugged into and connected to the source of power, God, we have no power on our own. This is similar to the metaphor of the vine:

> *I am the true vine, and my Father is the vine grower. He removes every branch in me that bears no fruit. Every branch that bears fruit he prunes to make it bear more fruit. John 15:1-3*

The leaves, the stems and the branches, on their own, have no power or life. It is only through their attachment to the plant, that they live. It is easy to mistake the life of the leaves as their own. Yet, as soon as they are cut off, they show their true nature. They begin to wither for, on their own, they have no power.

Similarly, on our own, we cannot make even one hair change its color:

> *And do not take an oath by your head, for you cannot make one hair white or black. Matt 5:36*

Once we realize this, we can put our ego aside and live

the powerful life. For if we insist that we have power on our own, we will be disappointed. We cannot add an inch to our height. We cannot grow one extra hair on our head. We cannot even exist on our own. Imagine us cut off from our environment. Without breathing, eating and drinking, we would not exist. For as long as we are connected to the source of power, we have power. Without the connection, we are powerless.

The most important power we have is that of life. The Syriac Aramaic **"haylo"** does not only mean power, it also means **might, energy, force, potency**, and **strength**. "**Haylo**" is intimately related to the word "**hayo**" which means **life**. Hence, by power we mostly mean the Vital Life Force coursing within us. It is this life force that gives us the appearance of life and power on our own.

By stating that God is the source of all power, we are admitting that even though it appears that we have power on our own, for we move and do things, our power comes from God. God is the source of life, potency, and power. We are the mere conduits to this power.

It is easy to remember this when we are faced with frailties. When we are sick, weak and incapacitated, we turn to God and pray asking for help and guidance. We realize that on our own, we are not mighty at all. We are a weakling. This is an occasion when we feel humble.

Once I had a terrible backache when I was home alone with no one to help. I could not move. It took me 45 minutes to crawl from my bed to the bathroom. It took real effort to put a pair of socks on my feet in preparation to go see a doctor. Times like these remind us clearly and definitively that, on our own, we are powerless.

For thine is the Glory *"Metool dilokhi Teshbuhto"*

As part of the temptation of Christ, the Devil showed Him the world with all of its glory and promised to give it all to Christ if only He would worship the Devil.

> *Then the devil led him up and showed him in an instant all the kingdoms of the world. And the devil said to him, "To you I will give their glory and all this authority; for it has been given over to me, and I give it to anyone I please. If you, then, will worship me, it will all be yours." Jesus answered him, "It is written, 'Worship the Lord your God, and serve only him.'" Luke 4:5-8*

Christ knew better. He passed the test and triumphed over the temptation because He clearly understood that only to God belongs glory. Glory did not belong to the Devil to give away. The Devil represents our ego and selfish nature. Hence acknowledging that on our own we have no glory, we too will triumph.

Forever and ever *"l olam olmin"*

Forever and ever means for all ages, throughout all time, world without end. In other words, always and on all dimensions. This fact will never change.

Elucidating via examples

We are an image

> *So God created humankind in his image, in the image of God he created them; male and female, he created them. Genesis 1:27*

The key word is *image*. We are created in the image of God. We are not God. While God is Almighty, has the Kingdom, the Power and the Glory, we are merely a reflection, a shadow of these. We reflect these because we are made in the image of God.

What does being in the image of God mean? Since this is a fundamental concept and vital to understand our true nature, I will use several examples to fully explain this concept.

1. The best way to understand the implication of what it means to be in the image of God is to stand in front of a mirror. When we look into a mirror what do we see? We see our image, right? Now try to move while you are still in front of the mirror. What do you notice? As you move, so does the image. The image appears to look just like you, but there are substantial differences. For one thing, you are 3-dimensional while the image is 2-dimensional. But the most important difference is that the image, even though it appears to move, does not have a life of its own. It does not have any power of volition. You move and the image appears to move, but the energy

comes from the real you and not from the image. You talk and the voice seems to come from the image, but the words are coming from you and not the image. For as long as the image stays connected to you, the image remains visible, moves and imitates you. Once the connection is severed, the image disappears and is no more. It is the same with us. Our life and power are from God. As long as we remain connected to our source, the I AM within us, we move and function. Sever the connection and we are dust and to dust we return.

2. Another simple way to understand what being an image of God is, is to look at a TV program. Imagine that you are watching a basketball game. You might forget yourself and get caught up in the game believing that what you are experiencing is real. You believe that the images are people, moving and shooting the basketball into the hoop. You hear the sounds, the voices, you see the action, and you imagine all this to be alive until someone pulls the electrical cord out of its socket and all of a sudden— all is gone. It was a mirage after all. The images where just that, *images*. They had no life of their own. They were mere reflections of the life and activity of the real people behind the scenes.

3. A third way to understand what it means to be an image of God is to look at a picture of ourselves. Even though the picture represents us and appears like us, it is not us. It is merely an image, a reflection of us. The picture is a shadow

of the person. It has no life of its own.

4. A fourth way to understand what it means to be an image of God is to look at a map. Even though the map represents territory, it is not real in the sense that where it shows a lake, there is no lake, only the position of a lake. The lake on the map is merely an image, a reflection of the reality of the earth on which it exists. The map is not the territory. It is a mere shadow of the real terrain. It has no value of its own without the reality of the earth it represents.

5. A final way to understand what being an image of God means is to look at a seed. A seed is in the image of the plant it came from. For example, a watermelon seed will become a watermelon once fully grown. It is the same with a pepper seed, an apple seed or an oak seed. Seeds grow to reflect their source. Seeds are not a replica of their source. A watermelon seed is not a watermelon until it is allowed to grow and manifest its destiny. So it is with us. As an image, we are potential. Once we unfold, grow and mature, then we reflect our source. We become real. We manifest the kingdom of God in our lives. Then, we have the kingdom, the power and the glory.

AMEN

Truth is a very different thing from fact; it is the loving contact of the soul with spiritual fact, vital and potent. It does not work in the soul independently of all faculty or qualification there for setting it forth or defending it. Truth in the inward parts is a power, not an opinion. — George MacDonald

It was not until I was reading the Syriac Aramaic version of the Bible that I came to know what "amen" means. Wherever the English version states: "verily, verily", or "truly, truly", the Aramaic words used are "ameen, ameen."

And he said to him, "Truly, truly, I say to you, you will see heaven opened, and the angels of God ascending and descending on the Son of Man." John 1:51

... "Ameem, ameen, omar no lkhoon",...

Amen is from the same root as "*eman*" which in Arabic means faith, belief, and being trustworthy. The Arabic "*eman*" and the Aramaic word for faith "*mhymno*" are both derived from "*amen.*"

Ending our prayer with **"amen"**, is giving our consent, agreement, assent, concord, and expressing full support to all that we stated previously. By ending our prayer with **"amen"**, we are agreeing and affirming that all that we stated in our prayer is the truth, the whole truth, and nothing but the truth. It is as if we are sealing our prayer with an affirmation of our faith, creed, understanding, and knowledge.

With "amen", we are sealing the "envelope" and "mailing" our prayer. We are letting it go. It now rests with God, our Father. We did our part. We have no attachment to outcome.

To recap

The Lord's Prayer is our Creed, our Affirmation of the Truth as we know it to be. Through this prayer we are making 10 affirmations of Truth:

1. First, we affirm our unity. There is **one** Father who is the source of all. We are all members of one family;

2. Second, we affirm that we can only Hallow God's name by honoring each other. For each is a name of God. Each is a **"neter"**, an aspect of God. We hollow the name of God best by recognizing the divinity within each;

3. Third, we affirm that by stating, **"Thy Kingdom Come!"** we are aspiring to realize this kingdom in our lives by striving to express who we are. We understand that we carry this Kingdom within

us as a seed which is in the process of unfolding. As our understanding matures and our consciousness rises to the Christ Consciousness, we manifest this kingdom in our lives with all of its glory. At this stage, the seed becomes the tree and the image becomes real, one with its source;

4. Fourth, we affirm that the will of God is our own highest desire. We also affirm that we are here on earth to discover and live the purpose for which we were born;

5. Fifth, we affirm that **our daily bread** is the challenges we face. It is our difficulties that force us to open our eyes and hearts. We begin to see clearer. We must learn to transform our challenges from obstacles into the spiritual nourishment that we need to grow and mature;

6. Sixth, we affirm that we are **forgiven to the extent that we ourselves forgive** and that it is up to us. If we release and let go, then it is done. By forgiving, we are automatically forgiven. There is no judgment or retribution;

7. Seventh, we affirm that if we are **led into temptation** then it is for our own good. Temptations are exactly what we need to grow, mature and realize our potential. Without temptations and the opportunity to overcome them, we cannot grow. Additionally, we affirm that we are not asking God *"not to Lead us into temptation"*. What we are asking instead is:

Oh God, please do not allow me to forget this

state I established by connecting to you. Do not allow me to forget who I am and become the Prodigal son. May I always remember why I am here on Earth and what it is that I came to do. Please do not let me forget that as long as I remain connected to you, I have the Kingdom, the Power and the Glory. Of my own, I have nothing and can do nothing.

8. Eighth, we affirm that we do not need to be **delivered from evil**. Rather, we need to confront and eliminate evil. Appearances can be deceiving. Being deceived by possessions, wealth and power as if they are real and lasting is the real Devil that we need to be delivered from. Instead of being delivered from evil, we need to face the evildoers and help them understand our unity;

9. Ninth, we affirm that humility is the name of the game. Even though we are a child of God, we are not to be glorified or adored. **The kingdom, the power, and the glory** belong only to God alone. God is real while we are a reflection, a mere shadow. Once we learn to function from our Higher Self allowing it to manifest its will through us, then the kingdom, power and glory become ours automatically;

10. Tenth, we affirm that by saying *"amen"*, we acknowledge that what we stated so far, is the truth, the whole truth and nothing but the truth.

◆ ◆ ◆

Personalizing the Lord's Prayer

Now that we know the hidden meaning and power of the Lord's Prayer based on its Syriac Aramaic, let us rewrite this prayer and personalize it based on our new understanding.

Please personalize this prayer to create your own version that means something special to you.

1. My source you are everywhere and in everything, especially in me.

2. Though you are invisible and in heaven, your handiwork is visible everywhere. I feel you in my beating heart.

3. You have implanted your abilities in me as a seed. This is my inheritance. I am in your image just as a picture of me is in my image. Guide me to actualize my potential and to transform the shadow that I am into the real that you are.

4. I am here for a purpose and a mission of my own choosing. Help me remember it and live to achieve it.

5. Help me open my eyes today, a bit wider than yesterday. May I see my experiences as the opportunities I need to learn from. May my pain and suffering tear away the veil that obstructs my vision and understanding. Help me to fearlessly express my unique individuality that you blessed me with as a special word with a unique name.

6. I know that as I forgive others, I myself am forgiven. If I let go, it is gone. I can start with a new slate

anytime I purge myself of the spent and unnecessary. I forgive myself and I forgive everyone else, now and always.

7. Please do not let me forget who I am and that I am always connected to you, my Father and my source. Help me remember this fact and live accordingly. Even more importantly, help me remember that so is everyone else. I Know that I am immature and am dealing with others who are immature just like me. Give me the patience, strength, and wisdom to always do my best with understanding and compassion until one day, I attain full maturity.

8. I am a mere image, a reflection, and a shadow. You are real. You are the source of all life, power and glory. If I consciously realize my connection to you, then I too can share in your life, your power, and your glory.

9. I attest to the truth of the above. These are my truths as I know them at this stage of my understanding. May I always remember that everyone else is entitled to their own version of this same Truth. Give me the wisdom to respect and appreciate these differences.

10. To you, I appeal with my prayer, now and always, Amen.

PART III

How to Pray for Results

12 Steps to Effective Prayer

HOW TO PRAY FOR RESULTS
12 Steps to Effective Prayer

One single grateful thought raised to heaven is the most perfect prayer. — G. E. Lessing

How do we know if our prayers are heard? Does God hear our actual words and understand our earthly language? How many languages does God know? If prayer is "an act of communion with God, or another object of worship," how does this communion take place? How do we establish contact with the deity? Does this communion take place some of the time or every time? Can we know when and if we have definitely established contact with the deity? Is there a certain feeling associated with this contact? In this section, we are going to learn:

1. How does prayer work?
2. What takes place in prayer?
3. How can we pray for results?
4. Where and how do the answers to our prayers come from?

At the beginning of this book, we discussed several types of prayers, among them:

1. Prayers of confession;
2. Prayers of supplication for intercession;
3. Prayers of adoration; and
4. Prayer as a statement of our creed, of what we believe in and know to be true.

Prayers of confession do not entail a reply, nor do prayers of adoration or creed. What requires a response is prayers of supplication for intercession. It is easy to fool ourselves by claiming that ALL of our prayers are always heard and answered. If we get what we asked for, we then say that God answered our prayers and granted us what we asked for. If, on the other hand, we do not get what we asked for, we then say that God heard our prayer and since God knows what is best for us, God decided not to grant us our request for our own good. This type of reasoning is mere justification. It is not proof that our prayers were heard or answered.

We can find out for sure if our prayers are heard and answered. We can test this system once we understand the mechanics of prayer. Before we delve into the mechanics of how prayer works, how it might be answered, and how we can test it, we need to state a few ground rules.

Ground rules of prayer

1. Prayer is not a game we play. God is not and cannot be a genie who grants us all we ask for. For one thing, we are not mature enough to know what is best for us. If

we get all that we ask for, it might be against our best interests. Like children, we might ask for candy until we get sick.

2. If every time we need something we run to God and ask for it, how are we to grow up and become self-sufficient? Those of us who have children know that we raise children to be independent and not depend on their parents for the rest of their lives. That is exactly how nature operates. Animals are weaned and pushed away to help them grow and be independent. We are expected to grow into self-sufficiency and take care of ourselves.

3. There is one God and this God is **everybody's** God and not just ours. There are no exceptions to this fact. In other words, this God cannot and will not favor one child over another. Hence, we cannot ask for something that rightfully belongs to someone else and expect God to favor us and take the item away from that person and give it to us. If, for example, we ask for a promotion and God grants us our wish, then a more deserving person will lose his or her chance for that position.

4. If we always get all that we need and want, life becomes too easy and loses its appeal. Boredom sets in and we lose our excitement and interest.

5. We need to develop confidence through self-reliance. Often, not getting something is an incentive to try harder, to be more determined and persist. We need to exercise our will power and be resolute. By not getting something we truly want, we can try harder and distinguish ourselves by excelling where others

give up. We are expected to do all we can for ourselves and only ask for help in cases where we have already done all we can possibly do and have exhausted all other avenues.

6. Instead of asking for things, we should instead ask for the knowledge of how and what to do ourselves. For example, instead of asking for a car, we should pray for the knowledge of what we can do to solve our transportation problem.

7. Lastly, instead of focusing on what we lack, we should be thankful for what we already have. Gratitude and appreciation are essential for our mental health and wellbeing. Having already received so many blessings, we should endeavor to give back in the form of service to others.

Praying for results

To understand the mechanics of how prayer works and how it gets answered, we need to first understand who we are praying to and how we are related to this divinity.

The explanations presented here are based on personal experience. My knowledge comes from my successes as well as from my failures. Do not accept anything at face value. Evaluate the material. Look into your own life to see if you can find correspondence with your own experiences. If you do, then accept the ideas and be thankful. Otherwise, try to understand the concepts and be patient. Do not judge hastily. Eventually you might have an experience that will cause you to change your mind. The answer often comes when we most need it

Briefly, there are only 3 fundamental concepts to understand:

1. First, there is a *field* in which all exist, move and function. It is like the atmosphere in which we live. It is like the ocean for the fish and the air for the birds. This field is holographic and permeates all. It is within and without us and is the medium that connects us all;

2. Second, the language of communication in this field is *energy*, specifically, emotional energy coupled with vivid visualization and imagination. The purer our emotions, the clearer our intentions and the stronger our desire (need), the more effective our prayer will be;

3. Finally, the more altruistic the request, the more likely that it will be granted.

Answers to prayers are not based on a whim, or are capricious. The "field" does not play favoritism. We have a major role in whether or not our prayers are answered. The mechanics of prayer is NOT a theory. It is a fact supported by science, metaphysics, spirituality and proven by personal experience.

When I was a student at the American University of Beirut, in Lebanon, and while studying physics, the following statement struck a chord within me and had a lasting impact. I never forgot it. Here is the statement:

No object can occupy space/time without distorting it to some degree. The amount of distortion depends on its charge.

In other words, we cannot be in space/time without distorting or impacting it in some way. How and to what extent we impact this field depends on our charge—the energy of our emotions and the state of our being.

To assure myself of the accuracy of the above statement, I referred back to my college textbook and found the following passage:

Fields Of Force

So far we have treated the gravitational attraction between masses as a direct interaction between the particles involved. Similarly, we have assumed that electric charges exert forces directly on each other. This kind of direct interaction between bodies is often called action at a distance. We shall now introduce a modification of this point of view that has proved to be enormously important in theory and very fruitful in application. In this modification we suppose that the space surrounding a mass (or charge) is somehow different from what it would be in the absence of the mass (or charge). In principle, this "distortion" extends throughout all space; in practice it often becomes quite negligible a short distance from the source mass or source charge. We call the distortion associated with mass a gravitational field and that associated with charge an electric field. This

> *distortion, or field, cannot be seen by the eye, but it is real nonetheless and can be measured.*
>
> **<u>A Contemporary View of Elementary Physics</u>**: *Borowitz and Bornstein, Chapter 5: The Kind of Forces Found in Nature*

Let us repeat the pertinent part of this passage once more for emphasis:

> *We suppose that the space surrounding a mass (or charge) is somehow different from what it would be in the absence of the mass (or charge). In principle, this "distortion" extends throughout all space; in practice it often becomes quite negligible a short distance from the source mass or source charge.*

In other words, whether we are aware of it or not, and whether we like it or not, the mere fact that we occupy space and time, we distort the energy field surrounding us and this energy field is the same energy field that contains all.

The implication of this statement is profound. By simply changing our charge through our emotions and mental framework, we change the nature of the field that holds us all. In other words, by simply changing ourselves, we impact the whole world, and all of existence. (the butterfly effect?) Obviously, the degree to which we influence this field depends on the clarity of our vision, purity of our intentions and the strength of our vibratory energy.

There is a third aspect to this field worth mentioning. This aspect is not as yet supported by science. It is, however, accepted by spirituality as true and factual.

A spiritual assertion:

This field is aware and intelligent and it responds in kind. It has no judgment and does not know good from evil. It is simply a mirror that reflects back to us what we project into it.

In other words, our attitudes, expectations and beliefs play a major role in determining the type of distortion we cause in the field. If our charge is "good", or "positive", then we affect this field in a good and positive way and good comes back to us. If, on the other hand, our charge is "negative", then we affect this field in a "bad" or negative way and the negative comes back to us as experiences. This is true whether or not we are conscious of this fact.

To summarize:

1. There is an energy field that we are immersed in and this field contains all;
2. We communicate with this field through our emotions and the state of our being;
3. This field responds in kind. What we put into it, comes back to us in kind. What we reap is in the image of what we have sown.

With this knowledge, we possess one of the greatest and most powerful insights anyone can have. What distinguishes humans from the gods, (as implied by the story of Adam and Eve), are knowledge and eternal life. We now possess some of the knowledge we need to transform ourselves from helpless and weak beings, into beings of power, light, knowledge and wisdom.

Knowledge, however, must not be theoretical and

intellectual. It must become experiential and instinctual before we reap the full benefits of this knowledge.

Earlier in the Lord's Prayer we discussed:

Thy will be done on earth as it is in heaven.

There is more to this statement than what is apparent. The order of the words is deliberate, intentional and is true only as it is stated. It's reverse, however, **"Thy will be done in heaven as it is on earth"** is not true for the following reason:

The doing takes place in Heaven while the results appear on Earth. Heaven leads while Earth follows. Heaven is the cause while Earth is the result. Heaven is where the "seeds" are sown and Earth is where the "plants" are reaped. Heaven is the field while our experiences are the result.

We are immersed in an energy field. This *field* of *energy* is expanded. We, however, are dense and contracted. Everything is either expanded or contracted—wave or particle. That which is expanded is "energy field" and is referred to as **Heaven**. Anything that is contracted is material and is referred to as **Earth**. While the "earthly" can be touched, felt and experienced, the "heavenly" eludes our senses.

Examples

1. The sky (heaven) is a vast expanse while earth, the moon, the sun and the other planets are condensed. The entire universe is of these two qualities: vast

expansion or what the ancients called: **heaven**, the void, the abyss, the darkness, the depth, profundity and what in Syriac Aramaic is called **"tehoomo"**. This is the word used in the Bible when God began creation. All that was, was this **"tehoomo"**, the void and the Abyss. Expansion, however, does not mean absence or true void. It simply means the space that holds, or contains the objects of our creations.

2. Material objects, on the other hand, are evident everywhere. They are around us and in the entire universe. They are scarce compared to the amount of "heaven" that surrounds us.

3. We, too, are of these two qualities. We have a physical and condensed body and we also have an expanded component, mind, consciousness and soul. While the condensed is subject to the senses, the expanded is not.

4. The atom, the building block of our universe, also has the two qualities of expansion and contraction. In the atom we have contracted objects such as protons, electrons and neutrons and we also have a tremendous amount of space, expansion and void. Relatively speaking, the atom is mostly empty space. The electrons, protons, and neutrons occupy only a tiny fraction of what constitutes the atom.

5. The photon is also wave and a particle. It is known as a wavicle. As a wave, it is expanded and as a particle, it is contracted.

Hence there are two distinct qualities to being:

    1. Manifest or condensed objects known as "Earth",

and
2. Unmanifest, potential, or expanded state, known as "Heaven."

The expanded is a field of energy. Energy is defined as *"the potential to do work."* Thus, this field of energy is *space imbued with unlimited potential.* While in this field, we can create, shape and manifest our hearts desire. This field is our playground to do our heart's bidding. **This is the field we find ourselves in.**

Even though we are immersed in this field of potential, what we do in this field, in Heaven, and while in touch with God—is based on how aware we are and the state of our being. The field of energy surrounding us is "God or our Father in Heaven." As we pray, we are earth surrounded by heaven. What we release while we are *in* Heaven, comes back to us, in the form of, or in the image of what we put out as hopes, desires, fears, expectations and beliefs.

This is how *"what we do in Heaven is done on Earth"* automatically and without judgment. Depending on the type of seeds we drop in this field, in this womb, corresponding results follow. As we sow, so shall we reap.

Worth remembering

Wherever we are, we are in the same field in which all else exists. We can influence this field by working on ourselves and by changing our charge through manipulating our emotions, attitude and state of being.

Relating this fact to prayer

If we want to have our prayers answered, we must do it in this field. Influencing the field is connecting to God and touching heaven. To do this correctly, we must **be** the state we desire and vibrate or radiate accordingly. This will create analogous vibrations in the field which will attract and return to us that which we send forth via intensely visualized desires, hopes and aspirations.

Recalling that God has three types of names; to get our prayers answered, we must use God's secret name. We must pronounce God's secret name by becoming that which we desire and wish for. The secret name of God, you may recall, is Being and I am. In other words, we must **be, not do**.

Therefore, we must **BE** that which we desire. As we become and are, we radiate accordingly. The field surrounding us changes to match our vibrations. The results we experience follow in accordance to the nature of the seeds we planted. What we get back is in the image of what we created by **being**. The same way that we are in the image of God, our creations are in our own image and after our likeness. Our experiences are not random. They are the "bread" we are asking for by being who we are, whether or not we are aware of this fact.

Cardinal fact

> *We are always connected to our Father. Always. We never break away from our Father except through our lack of awareness and by choice. To the extent that we are aware of our connection, we are connected. Once our awareness wavers and we are no longer focused on our connection, then we are no longer connected to our Father in the sense that we*

are not aware of our connection even though we are still connected. We can never be outside this field in which we, and in which all else are immersed.

It is all a matter of where we place our awareness. Allowing our Higher Self to express itself through us, our connection is permanent. If we allow our selfish ego to run our lives, we are no longer aware of our connection. This is like holding a pencil in our hands for a long time. After a while, we forget that we have the pencil. The same is true with the clothes we wear. We are not aware that we have them on, even though they are touching our bodies at all times. Similarly, we are not aware of the hair on our head, until we are. If we make a conscious effort to be aware, we establish the connection. Hence, unless we place our awareness on something, we are not aware of that thing. This is the nature of our reality. Since we can only focus on one item or one group at a time, we forget all except the object of our current attention.

To remind ourselves of our connection to our Father, we go to a place of worship or we participate in a ritual. When we pray, we usually intentionally focus our awareness on God and thus reestablish our connection. Ritual and places of worship enhance our awareness of our connection to our Father. Focusing on the selfish self and the ego is a sure way to forget our connection to the divine within. Hence, the best way to remain connected to our Father, the divine within, is to live a moral, spiritual, kind and loving life.

Application

Unapplied knowledge is useless. Application is the key to transform theoretical information into experiential knowledge. One of the best ways to test this theory and find out if our prayers get answered is to pray for something unusual that leaves no room for guessing or imagining that we received an answer. We know our prayer was answered if the source of the answer was far superior to our own capability. I would like to share a personal experience of how I used my knowledge of effective prayer to attract into my life what I needed most at the time.

The most important person in a married person's life is their spouse. How I met my wife was a direct answer to my prayer. Since I wrote about this in my book, **A Passion for Living**, *a path to meaning and joy*, I will use a direct quote from that book:

Finding Barbara

> *"I had mostly lived a lonely life in Lebanon. Except for the occasional visits with my friends and Aunt Faith, I was mostly alone. I was 24 years old when I entered the United States in 1972 on Valentine's Day. In July of 1972, I joined the U. S. Army for a three-year tour of duty.*
>
> *Throughout my tour in the Army, I was lonely and in search of a companion and mate. I unsuccessfully struggled through the efforts of dating and even offered to marry a childhood friend in Lebanon. All to no avail.*
>
> *It was now February 1976, and I was still alone and lonely. Out of desperation, I decided to employ a combination of prayer and meditation to plead my case to the Cosmic Hosts and ask for help. I knew*

exactly what I wanted—to attract the one most suitable to be my friend and mate. I felt deserving and my intentions were clear. I prepared myself and entered into a meditative state. I was in a highly charged emotional state. I raised my consciousness until I felt I was in the presence of the Cosmic Intelligence. I pleaded my case vividly, intensely and passionately. I asked for help and guidance. I requested a solution to my loneliness. I declared my readiness to meet my mate. I then expressed gratitude and slowly reverted back to my normal state. As soon as I was back, I knew beyond any shadow of doubt that I had made contact and that my plea was heard and answered. My request would soon manifest in physical reality.

In April of 1976, the local Rosicrucians held a class in one of the hotels in downtown Washington, DC. I decided to take this class. After walking into the room, I looked around to see who was there. All of a sudden, my heart started to pound loud and fast and a clear voice from deep within thundered forth: "the one you seek is here." Looking at her, our eyes met. I knew she was the one. I walked over and asked if she would have dinner with me that Friday night. She agreed and gave me her address and phone number on a piece of paper.

I had met Barbara earlier, the first time in November of 1975, during the intermission of a Rosicrucian play I was taking part in. I talked with her then, casually. She looked shy and old fashioned, yet bright and friendly. She was wearing a long colorful gown. She asked me many questions about myself. When I met her again, I was surprised that she remembered everything about me, while I could not even remember her name.

I wondered why I felt the way I did when I saw her this time. I decided to accept the feeling and go with it. Meanwhile, Barbara was wondering why she had accepted my invitation so readily and whether or not she should call to cancel. Fortunately, she did not have my phone number.

I picked Barbara up from her apartment in Arlington, Va. and drove her to my apartment in Glen Burnie, Md. where I had prepared stuffed grape leaves for dinner and fresh strawberries for dessert. While driving her back to her apartment later that night, she fell asleep in the car. I stopped the car, got a blanket from the trunk and covered her up. I knew Barbara was going to be my wife. It took Barbara a few weeks to even let me hold her hand.

I asked and received a gift. I knocked and a door opened. Yet, at no time was I forced to accept the gift or walk through the door. These were my decisions. Trusting in an intelligence far higher than mine that knows what is best for me, I gratefully accepted the gift. We have been happily married for over twenty years and have two daughters, Olivia and Emily. I have never met anyone whom I would rather have for a wife. Barbara has been perfect for me and, hopefully, I for her."

By using a successful mentor, we can learn from them to

be successful ourselves. Similarly, by using the method I used to get my prayer answered, we can extract the steps necessary for effective prayer.

12 steps to effective prayer

1. Out of desperation, I decided to employ a combination of prayer and meditation to plead my case to the Cosmic Hosts (God) and ask for help.
2. I felt deserving.
3. My intentions were clear.
4. I prepared myself.
5. I entered into a meditative state.
6. I was in a highly charged state. I raised my consciousness until I felt I was in the presence of the Cosmic Intelligence (God).
7. I pleaded my case vividly, intensely and passionately.
8. I asked for help and guidance. I requested a solution to my loneliness.
9. I declared my readiness to take action so I can meet my mate.
10. I then expressed gratitude.
11. I slowly reverted back to my normal state.
12. As soon as I was back, I *knew* beyond any shadow of doubt that I had made contact and that my plea was heard and answered. My request would soon manifest in physical reality. I was confident and elated.

1. Out of desperation, I decided to employ a combination of prayer and meditation to plead my case to the Cosmic Hosts (God) and ask for help. It is important to realize that I did everything in my power to solve the problem on my own beforehand, without success. I did not appeal to God for help until it became the last resort. I dated several young ladies while at Ft. Meade. I even wrote a letter asking for the hand of a young lady I knew in Beirut, Lebanon, all to no avail. I was lonely and needed companionship.

2. I felt deserving. I knew and believed beyond any shadow of a doubt that what I was asking for, I deserved and needed. It was something that I had to have. It was something I could not do without. Yet I was ready to give in return. We had to be right for each other. Even though the benefit I was seeking was for myself, it was not selfish. I was looking for love, companionship and normalcy which is the right of every human being. We deserve to be happy. We cannot be productive and contribute our best otherwise.

3. My intentions were clear. There was nothing ambiguous about what I was asking. It was all clear in my mind and heart. I was focused on one single goal that I was seeking help with. I was asking to attract the one most suitable to be my companion and mate so we grow and mature together. How and what we ask for might be self-evident but bears emphasis. It must be clear and specific. There can be no conflicting views about what we want. I knew exactly what I

wanted—in **qualities**. I did not state or visualizes any physical features of the person. I was looking for someone with whom I could grow spiritually.

4. I prepared myself. I went through a ritual of preparation prior to praying. I washed my hands and face and got mentally and emotionally ready. I even changed my clothes. I entered my room and locked the door. I might have lit a candle and burnt some incense to create the right atmosphere.

5. I entered into a meditative state. I cleared my mind and heart of everything except of the desire to connect with God my Father. I was focused on establishing contact.

6. I was in a highly charged state. I raised my consciousness until I felt I was in the presence of the Cosmic Intelligence (God).

7. I pleaded my case vividly, intensely and passionately. I did not use words. I expressed my intentions, desires and needs in vivid pictures and live scenes. I did not visualize the person I wanted in any details or features. I only wanted the one with whom I would grow spiritually and build a fruitful life together.

8. I asked for help and guidance. I requested a solution to my loneliness. I asked for what I should do, where I should go and how I should proceed. I knew I could not be given anything other than the guidance I needed on what to do to get what I wanted. I pleaded: "show me the way. What is my next move"?

9. I declared my readiness to do my part. I was ready to act once I knew what I should do.

10. Here is where I saw myself, in my mind's eye, transformed, happy and with the one I loved. I bathed my being with this wonderful feeling. I then expressed gratitude, thanked God and firmly stated: "Thy will be done."

11. As soon as *I knew* that my wishes were received and that my request had been granted, I was overwhelmed with a sense of joy and appreciation. Slowly, I reverted back to my normal state.

12. As soon as I was back, I *knew* beyond any shadow of doubt that I had made contact and that my plea was heard and answered. My request would soon manifest in physical reality. I let go of all thoughts regarding this issue. I, then went on with my normal activities.

Knowing that I had made contact, that my prayer was heard and would soon be answered is a feeling I can never forget. It is impossible to fake this. My request as a *"seed"* was dropped into the fertile soil of the field, or *"heaven."* It is only a matter of time before it sprouts and manifests as physical reality on *"earth"* and in my life.

This formula can help us receive the answers we seek from our prayers. It worked for me and I am sure it will work for you. What we need to keep in mind is that God the Father will never grant us anything if we do not first ask. We can only ask after we try all that is within our power to do ourselves. And even after we ask, we are expected to act and make the results happen once we receive the guidance as to what we need to do next. When we ask, we ask best by **"*becoming*"** that which we seek. We assume the role and play the part as if we already have what we seek.

Christ makes it clear that we must knock before any door will be opened for us. Since we have free will, unless we ask, God will never interfere in our lives. We have the right to live our lives anyway we see fit. It is only after we ask that we can receive help and guidance since this does not invalidate our freedom of choice. We must first knock before any door opens for us.

> *Ask, and it will be given you; search, and you will find; knock, and the door will be opened for you. For everyone who asks receives, and everyone who searches finds, and for everyone who knocks, the door will be opened. Matt 7:7-8*

We must take the first step. We must ask, seek and knock. We must initiate the process. We must be willing to meet God halfway. If we want it, we must go after it. We must be proactive. We cannot lie idly and wait for things to fall into our laps. We must be doers and initiators.

Once we ask and are shown what to do, it is up to us to accept the offer and act or refuse it and do nothing. In the final analysis it is up to us. We must seize the moment and the opportunity afforded us. We cannot doubt, be timid or afraid. We must boldly respond with appreciation for the opportunity. We must act or else we will waste our chance.

> *Lose this day loitering, it will be the same story tomorrow, and the rest more dilatory; Thus*

indecision brings its own delays and days are lost tormenting over days.

Are you in earnest? Seize this very minute; what you can do or dream you can, begin it. Boldness has genius, power and magic in it; Only engage and then the mind grows heated;

Begin and then the work will be completed." Goethe

How and where do the answers come from?

Answers to our prayers can come while we are awake or asleep through a dream. It can come from within or without us, from someone else. It can be in clear terms or cloaked in symbolism.

In my book, **A Passion for Living, a path to meaning and joy,** I write about another request I made to the God. This was an ongoing "prayer" for me. I would complain to God, my Father about my situation. "Why do I have to go to this boring job, day after day, wait for a paycheck when I can be doing something more valuable such as writing, teaching and making a difference in the lives of others"? "Why I am stuck working for a living instead of functioning at a higher level and enjoying my accomplishment"? "How can I move from where I am and be where I can use more of my creativity"?

The answer came to me in a dream:

> I began having a recurring dream. In this dream, I live in a house. There is nothing outstanding about

this house except that somewhere beneath the house, I discover a large hole leading to a passage. I follow the passage. It gets progressively wider as it snakes itself deep underneath the house. Soon I arrive at a wide opening. At this opening I see a beautiful sight—caverns studded with colorful stalagmites and stalactites forming some of the most exquisite figurines and statuettes that I have ever seen. As I walk back up to the house, I see large crowds outside waiting to visit my caverns. However, there is no developed pathway leading to the caverns.

I had to "see" this dream many times before I understood its meaning. I did not need something new to attain my heart's desires. I did not have to travel far to arrive at what I sought. I already had what I needed in the form of "rough diamonds." The house in my dream was my mind. If I dug deep inside of it, I would unearth treasures in the form of ideas that could provide me with what I was searching for. I just had to develop these ideas and make them beautiful enough for people to want to "visit" them. Even though what I had to start with was a mere glitter in my eyes, I was sitting on a gold mine. I was the owner of the farm full of diamonds in the rough. With this insight, I saw exactly what I was to do next. I must pave a way for people to visit my caverns. I needed to transform the ordinary stones I had into precious stones. Clear insight propelled me into action. I began to think and write. The idea of a book was born. I worked diligently writing my first book, **A Passion for Living, a path to meaning and joy.** This was my first paved road to my caverns. More soon followed.

We do not pray only when we are in a house of worship, kneeling down, or next to our bed before we go to sleep. We pray anytime and anywhere when we seek and establish communion with Our Father, God. We pray through our emotions, desires, visions, intentions, attitudes, expectations, beliefs and knowledge. Praying with our entire being is the most effective way to pray.

We are always praying and we do not know it. Sadly, we do not always pray for "good and beneficial things." Most of what we experience is the result of our subconscious prayers which are negative and harmful.

We are like a radio or television tower always transmitting to the "field", God our Father, our deepest hopes, fears, aspirations, apprehensions, loves and hates. It matters not to God what we transmit. What we receive is always according to what we transmit.

Having free will is a major responsibility for we can and often do choose to bring hardships and calamities upon ourselves. We attract, not what we want, but rather what we need and we are seldom aware of the causes we are putting in motion. Soon the results follow and we wonder why. "Why is this happening to me, we ask?" The question to ask is not why it is happening to me but rather; since it is happening to me, what can I do about it? What good can I derive from it? How can I transform it? What can I learn from it? How can I use it to help others? And more importantly, how and why did I attract this situation? In other words, what am I transmitting and what is my state of being?

We are much more powerful than we are aware, especially if we know how to stay connected to our source, the field and God, our Father.

PART IV

How to Re-enter the Kingdom of Heaven

A spiritual perspective

HOW TO RE-ENTER THE KINGDOM OF HEAVEN

A Spiritual Perspective

Your job is to be you, which includes being the chief beneficiary of all things you do right, the chief victim of all you do wrong, and the one person on Earth who has to live with every choice you make. As gatekeeper to your life, you're it. – Carolyn Hax

Religion is meant to show us the way to God. It teaches us what we must do to earn a great afterlife, ensure a state of bliss and a heaven or a paradise to reside in forever. These are something to look forward to and something to strive for.

If we abide by the creeds of Christianity, then we are assured salvation and an eternal life in Paradise. If we follow the tenets of Islam, then we are assured paradise as well. These tenets include affirmation of faith, prayer, fasting, giving alms, good deeds and pilgrimage.

Buddhism, on the other hand, offers options. One can choose between several paths to attain Nirvana according to one's inclination. Each path is a discipline and is known as yoga. Thus, one can travel the path of good works, effort or discipline, devotion, meditation, posture and behavior, any one of which can lead to Nirvana.

The object of religion, whether it is heaven, Nirvana, Paradise, or the return to the Garden of Eden is basically the same. It is a return to a spiritual state, free of suffering, toil, and mortality. Unfortunately, one must wait until after death to discover the validity of what religion promulgates.

Spirituality on the other hand, enables us to attain the state we desire while still alive and in a physical body. This requires action based on specific knowledge. The knowledge is often referred to as Sophia, or Gnosis. This knowledge is not easy to come by. To discover it, one must learn to see beyond the language of symbolism, allegory, and parables. Once this knowledge is acquired, however, it must be placed in a "cauldron" where it is incubated, and then it must be sublimated or fermented until a transformation takes place. With transformation comes a change in phase and the Philosopher's stone is fashioned. With this stone in hand, one can turn "lead" into "gold" and achieve one's objectives.

Other terms for The Philosopher's Stone are The Elixir of Life, Fountain of Youth, The Magic Wand, Paradise, Heaven, The Kingdom of God or The Kingdom of Heaven. The object of both spirituality and religion is to possess this magical transforming agent (knowledge) and to return to a state we once had. While religion states the path clearly, spirituality hides it in allegory, symbolism and parables. While most religions tell us what we must do, believe, obey and follow, giving us a "fish", spirituality forces us to discover the answer ourself. It teaches us how to fish. For once we possess the knowledge, we are assured entrance to the state we desire and no one can take that away from us. In religion, one is at the mercy of others. We are either given access to Paradise or denied entrance. Spirituality places our destiny in our own hands. We are responsible and are held accountable for our lives. If we want Paradise, we must find the way ourselves.

Since humans were once in Paradise, perhaps by re-examining the story of Adam and Eve in the Garden of Eden afresh, will show us the way back.

According to the Old Testament, we were once in a paradise, a Garden of Eden, innocent and pure. We had all we needed. Then, due to disobedience, we were expelled from Paradise. What is more, we were prevented from returning to our lost state. The question is: "Is it possible to go back to our original state?"

For those who believe in a physical Garden of Eden and a literal Paradise, they will have to wait until after death to find out. What follows is for those who understand that there is a symbolic and an allegorical meaning to the story of the Garden of Eden.

The Garden of Eden as an allegory

The cast

1. **Adam**
   From *Adamu*, the Sumero-Babylonian version of the first man. Adam is earth, clay, or a being who has blood in him, (a *dam*, a=with, *dam*= blood). Adam represents the male human.

2. **Eve**
   From the Syriac Aramaic and Hebrew root *"hwh"*, (*he, vau, he*) meaning life. *"hwh"* transcribed into Latin letters becomes *"Eve."* Eve is the mother of all the living. Eve represents the life giver, the one who gives birth. Eve represents the female human.

3. **Serpent**
   The symbol for wisdom, knowledge and understanding. The serpent represents our accumulated experiences and the knowledge gained from them. These act as the impetus for our actions.

   > *Behold, I am sending you out as sheep in the midst of wolves, so be wise as serpents and innocent as doves. Matt 10:16*

4. **God of the Old Testament**
   Represents the external forces acting on us. Authority figures telling us what we can do and what we cannot do, what is acceptable and what is not, what is condoned and what is not. This could range from our parents, to religion, to science or to any authority figure.

5. **Two trees**
   Tree of Life: The source of our life which for the ancients was the ***heart***.
   Tree of knowing: (good and evil). The object of discernment, hence the ***mind***.
   Good: That which aids our unfoldment, evolution and advancement.

Evil: That which hinders our progress.

6. **Center of the Garden**
There can only be one item at a center. Since both trees were at the center, we are to understand that these two trees are entangled and must always function together. The mind reasons while the heart intuits and feels.

Garden

The root word, *Gen*, (from **Genna**) means a field or an enclosure. The garden represents life on earth and its circumstances. Moreover, a garden is:

A. **Orderly, organized,** and **tended for** usually by a gardener;
B. A harmonious amalgamation of desired entities coexisting and benefiting each other;
C. A *cultivated* piece of land used to grow what is desirable. The American Heritage Dictionary defines cultivation as:

  a. To improve and prepare (land), as by plowing or fertilizing, for raising crops; till. **b.** To loosen or dig soil around (growing plants);
  b. To grow or tend (a plant or crop);
  c. To promote the growth of (a biological culture);
  d. To nurture; foster;
  e. To form and refine, as by education;
  f. To seek the acquaintance or goodwill of; make friends with.

Our life as a garden

A garden can contain flowering or berry-bearing shrubs, ornamental or fruit bearing trees, vegetables, herbs, and an assortment of animals such as bees, butterflies, worms, birds and other varieties of fauna and flora. The key for having a garden is **the order, or harmonious coexistence and the desirability of all that exist in the garden.** The gardener is the *cultivator* who takes care of the garden by tilling the ground, nurturing, weeding out the undesirable, and by feeding the desirable. We are the gardeners. We must ever be alert as to what is growing in our garden.

The seeds dropped in a garden are carefully selected. A garden is not a haphazard mishmash of unrelated entities. If a "weed" seed falls into the garden and begins to grow, the gardener uproots the weed and tosses it out of the garden. It does not belong in the garden. To re-enter the Kingdom of Heaven, we must transform our minds and lives into a garden. While we cannot go back to the Garden of Eden, we can create it in our lives.

While the garden is our life, the soil of our garden is the fertile mind/heart. The seeds carefully selected and allowed to grow are our thoughts nurtured by our emotions. The gardener is the gatekeeper and it is our conscious mind. Hence, we must ever be vigilant to weed and feed this garden so only the desired fauna and flora prosper while the weeds are eradicated or deprived nourishment and are made to wither away and die.

Our two trees in the middle of our garden, the heart and

the mind, must always be at the center, entangled and working together. We cannot be all mind or all heart. We must master using reason and intuition together, the one complementing the other.

It is not good to be alone

> Then the LORD God said, "It is not good that the man should be alone; I will make him a helper fit for him." Gen 2:18

We cannot function well by ourselves. We need others to interact with. In this case, Adam and Eve represent the complete human. It takes two to interact, socialize, and grow. Eve is not only Adam's companion, she is also his wife, soulmate, and partner. Together, they can create, build, and progress. We are social beings. We must master balancing privacy with sociability, being alone and being with others.

In one version, Adam and Eve were created together as one entity, both male and female. In other words, Adam and Eve represent the dual aspect of each human. While Adam is the masculine, Eve is the feminine. We are both masculine and feminine at the same time. We need to master using both aspects to create a Garden of Eden in our lives. We need to learn when to be firm and resolute and when to be flexible and compassionate.

Free Will

Adam and Eve had a choice, a decision to make —obey or disobey. Adam representing mind and reason, abstained. Eve, representing heart and intuition, acted.

> *So when the woman saw that the tree was good for food, and that it was a delight to the eyes, and that the tree was to be desired to make one wise, she took of its fruit and ate, and she also gave some to her husband who was with her, and he ate. Then the eyes of both were opened, and they knew that they were naked. And they sewed fig leaves together and made themselves loincloths.*
> Gen 3:6-7

Eve's decision was not impulsive. She did not simply yield to temptation. She desired wisdom, knowledge and the ability to see clearly. She wanted to decide for herself, accepted the consequences of her decision and acted wisely.

The story of Adam and Eve in the Garden of Eden is the story of choice and the exercise of Free Will. Free Will is one of the most precious gifts that we have. To not use it, is an insult to the gift giver. Even though we are led to believe that we can act in only one way and that is to carry out the "orders" of an authority figure, that is not true. There can never be true Free Will if we are not allowed to choose. We are free to decide and to act according to the dictates of our conscience. Our choice is to obey external authorities or to listen to the Voice Within and act accordingly. Whatever we decide, we must accept the consequences.

The Serpent

The serpent, representing wisdom impelled Eve to act. There is no nobler incentive to act than to acquire wisdom and understanding. This is exactly what

Solomon asked for:

> At Gibeon the LORD appeared to Solomon in a dream by night, and God said, "Ask what I shall give you." And Solomon said, " ... Give your servant therefore an understanding mind to govern your people, that I may discern between good and evil, for who is able to govern this your great people?" 1 King 3:5-9

It is evident that the serpent was telling the truth to Eve, " ...you shall not die, your eyes will open and you will become like god knowing good from evil." Their eyes did open, they acquired wisdom and they did not die. In fact, Adam lived to an old age of 930 years:

> Thus all the days that Adam lived were 930 years, and he died. Gen 5:5

It is in the nature of the serpent to outgrow its limiting skin. We must emulate the serpent in adopting continuous growth and the shedding the skin of our ignorance and limiting beliefs.

The four rivers of the garden

There were four rivers in the Garden of Eden to water the soil. Our soil is our mind and its fertility depends on the nature of what is **"*watering*"** it. The four rivers flowing in the midst of our garden are habits, attitudes, expectations and beliefs. These are what waters our minds. Repeated actions give rise to habits, which over time give rise to attitudes, which in turn form our expectations and beliefs. Hence, it is vital to form appropriate habits.

Rays of sunshine and bursts of creativity invigorate the life of our garden. We must spray our garden with the water of our passions and add fertilizers in the form of hopes, dreams and aspirations. We can employ visualization on a regular basis to kindle our desires.

While we live in the world, the world lives within our minds. Our minds are like plots of land. Our minds can be gardens or waste lands. Each mind has many plants growing in it. Many people allow weeds to grow in their minds. If these weeds take over, they will hide and suffocate the good plants, the ones that bear abundant fruit. We all have some weeds in our gardens hiding among the good plants. Weeds grow naturally. It takes effort, care and dedication to have a healthy, productive garden. We must learn how to be effective gardeners by weeding the undesirables and feeding the favored. We must become cultivators of our minds.

What happens when we know

Eating of the *"tree"*, is experiencing. Experience leads to knowing. Knowing results in the following:

1. The opening of the eyes;
2. Knowing good from evil;
3. Becoming like God.

Opening of the eyes

> *for God doth know that in the day ye eat thereof, then your eyes shall be opened, and ye shall be as God, knowing good and evil. Gen 3:5*

When our eyes open, we see clearly, we know and

we understand. We become like God knowing Good from Evil. We acquire discrimination. We realize our "nakedness" lack and of culture and sophistication. Our eyes, however, open gradually. Once we have enough "lessons-learned", we undergo a change in phase. We jump into a higher quanta and we become transformed.

Knowing Good from Evil

This requires discrimination, judgment, and evaluation. It is to have the ability to distinguish, not only between the obvious Good and Evil, but the not so obvious as well. In other words, we cannot be fooled by appearance. We must go beyond the obvious to determine the true value of an experience over a long period of time.

The boundary between Good and Evil is not clear. It is easy to distinguish between Good and Evil at their extremes. It is the grey areas that give us trouble. What might start out being good can end up being evil. For example, was my mother's early death good or evil? Initially, it was the worst that could befall us. In the long run, however, it was a blessing in disguise. It is what set us free to seek new lives.

I have always trusted people. My motto has been: "If you have no reason to mistrust someone, then you should trust them until they give you a reason not to trust them anymore." This philosophy worked well until I encountered con artists who were out to defraud and take advantage of me. Now that I have been conned and taken advantage of, I have a new motto: "Trust people only after you know them and look out for con artists." There is no good or evil independent of circumstance. We must experience evil to know good.

Becoming like God

We are not like God. We are in the image of God.

> *Then God said, "Let us make man in our image, after our likeness. And let them have dominion over the fish of the sea and over the birds of the heavens and over the livestock and over all the earth and over every creeping thing that creeps on the earth." So God created man in his own image, in the image of God he created him; male and female he created them. Gen 1:26-28*

The key word is *"image"*. We are in the image of God. We are not like God. For a detailed description of what it means to be in the image of God, please refer to the section in this book titled, **"For thine is the kingdom, power and glory."**

The Cherub

> *therefore the LORD God sent him out from the garden of Eden to work the ground from which he was taken. He drove out the man, and at the east of the garden of Eden he placed the cherubim and a flaming sword that turned every way to guard the way to the tree of life. Gen 3:23-24*

To re-enter the Garden of Eden, we must go past the cherub guarding the entrance. Let us take a closer look at how we can do that.

1. **The entrance is at the east**. The sun, symbol of enlightenment, understanding, and knowledge rises in the east. This implies that the entrance requires a specific knowledge since east is

symbolic of enlightenment.

2. **The entrance is guarded by the cherubim.** Cherubim is the plural of cherub. Cherub is from the Syriac Aramaic "***kroobo***" which means to plow, to till the fallow ground. In other words, the cherub refers to tilling or cultivating the mind/heart in preparation for planting. To cultivate is to till, or to turn over. What we need to turn over are our attitudes. The presence of the cherub implies that we must become cultivators of the mind/heart. We must become proficient gardeners weeding the undesirable and feeding the desirable. We must selectively plant seeds we want to grow into habits, attitudes and beliefs that serve us and that foster our maturation. We must master employing the higher faculties of mind such as visualization, imagination, inspiration, contemplation and meditation. At the same time, we must express the finer emotions of love, sympathy and empathy. These are the tools that will aid us to create Paradise in our daily lives.

3. **The cherub is guarding the entrance with a flaming sword that turns every way.** The sword is symbolic of will and resoluteness. In other words, we must be decisive and firm on the choices we make and the life we choose to live. We cannot tarry, meander and be non-committed. We must be doers. We must act decisively and without fear.

Question

What seeds must we foster, plant and nurture?

In the soil of our minds/hearts, we selectively nurture the seeds that we want to develop into habits that serve us. According to *William James,* our greatest transforming agent is our mind and by: **"changing the inner attitude of our minds, we can change the outer aspects of our lives".** We determine the quality of our lives by the thoughts we entertain and the attitudes we harbor.

In the deepest soil of our mind/heart, there is one seed we need to be concerned with above all else. This seed is beyond value. It is the essence of who we are. It is our soul. This soul is in the form of a seed that unless we nurture it and allow it to grow, we will not survive death. A seed has three characteristics:

1. It is condensed potential and is in the image and likeness of its source. An apple seed, when it grows and matures will become like its source—an apple tree. A seed also has the potential to add to its inherited abilities as it experiences, grows and matures;

2. A seed is a dormant life entity. Once planted, it responds to its environment, grows and expresses its individuality;

3. A seed has intelligence. It attracts to itself what it needs to grow and unfold. As it grows, it begins to display the source from which it originated. It also accumulated new experiences.

Similarly, soul has 3 features:

1. It is condensed potential in the image and

likeness of its Source. Each soul is a unique Image, Idea, Word, and Identity that God had in mind from the beginning. As we were released from the Mind of God, we were endowed with free will to seek the manner of our unfoldment, growth and maturation. We can take the short road and be on an accelerated path, or we can take the long road. We can go either way as long as we do not stagnate and refuse to grow;

2. It animates the body with life, mind and consciousness. The body lives while it houses the soul. The body dies as soon as the soul departs;

3. It has intelligence. Our soul will attract to us the circumstances we need to grow and mature. These are often challenges we must overcome and obstacles that we must transform into opportunities so we can gain mastery. Our soul also arranges synchronicities for us to take advantage of and shorten the path to full growth and maturation.

Our soul gives us our unique identity. It houses our character and personality. It is our spiritual DNA. Initially, as soul, it is perfect and in the image of its Source, God. As we live and experience, we deposit on this pristine soul our accumulated memories and distort the original image into something of our own making. It reflects the choices we have made and the actions we have taken. What we add to soul is epi-soul. Over time, the original Idea, Image and Word become personalized, a reflection of us instead of God. This is because of our freedom of choice. Once we learn to make the "right" choices, our development will accelerate until we finally reflect our mature, divine nature.

What do we need to know?

If knowing opens our eyes to see clearly and to understand, what is the primary knowledge that we need to have?

THE SECRET OF CHRISTIANITY

There are several powerful verses in the New Testament. One of the most important verses and the one that distinguishes Christianity from all other religions is the following:

> *Jesus answered them, "Destroy this temple, and in three days I will raise it up." John 2:19*

This statement demonstrates that Jesus knew exactly who he was. He was the one who fashions, molds, and shapes his physical body. He knew that He was a living soul in a physical body. He was the power, the life and the intelligence that resides in and animates the body. Destroy the body and He can rebuild it. This is the kind of knowledge that we need. We need to know that:

1. We are A LIVING SOUL. We are the Farmer using the seed, the Merchant owning the pearl, the Fisherman casting the net;
2. We are Love, Beauty and Joy;
3. We are an aspect of the divine, connected, and ONE with our source—God;
4. Our soul as seed endows us with vast potential. We can never exhaust actualizing our potential.

In the Garden of Eden

Once in the Garden of Eden, we find ourselves fully awake. Simultaneous with our waking up we realize that:

1. We are always where we need to be;
2. We have what it takes to achieve whatever we set our sights on;
3. We never have to struggle to succeed;
4. Everyone and everything matter, and
5. We are all connected forming one gigantic family.

CONCLUSION

I hope by now it is obvious why Christ wanted us to recite this particular prayer—we are to have a new concept of God, a concept that ennobles and empowers us. Instead of a god of jealousy, vengeance and mean spiritedness, we now have a parent as our God. We do not need intermediaries to have access to our Father. Yet this Father will never, ever favor us over another. He will never, ever set aside natural laws to please us. He will never grant us our wishes if they, in any way, might harm or disadvantage another.

We have been gifted with free will. We are expected to use it to create the life we desire for ourselves and for our loved ones. We cannot indulge ourselves to excess, get sick and then pray for health. We must do what we can ourselves, first. We are much more capable than we realize. Our focus should be, "What can I do right now?" "What is within my power to accomplish on my own?" We should not pray asking for things we can do for ourselves. Most of our prayers should be expressions of gratitude for what we already have.

Our father does not dwell in faraway place, a heaven. He is within us as a seed that we need to nurture and cultivate. Our Father is the embodiment of Love, Beauty and Joy.

Our Father is Love. Anytime we love selflessly, we feel God

in our hearts and we see "Him" in the ones we love.

Our Father is Beauty. Anytime we are moved by beauty, we feel our Father in our hearts and we see "Him" in all the expressions beauty manifests itself through.

Our Father is Joy. Anytime we feel joy, we experience God and we see "Him" in the ones who allow us to experience joy through them.

The old god is dead. Long live the new God, the God of Love, Beauty and Joy.

APPENDIX

*How one book altered
the course of my life*

HOW ONE BOOK ALTERED THE COURSE OF MY LIFE

Books don't change the world, people change the world, books only change people. — Mario Quintana

Soon after I was stationed at Ft. Meade, Md, I befriended a man from Chicago, IL. His name was J. T. One day, out of the blue, J. T offered me a book as a gift. This book was, **The Greatest Salesman in the World** by Og Mandino. I, not only read the book, but I applied the principles stated in the book to my life. In the ensuing months, I purchased and gave away multiple copies of this same book to various people. Since this one book altered the course of my life for the better, I wanted to do the same for as many people as I could. I would like to acquaint you with seven books, any one of which can do the same for you and anyone else you care about.

I have labored long and hard to find answers to the perplexing questions of life. My persistence to know inspired me to find answers that satisfy. I made many discoveries, and in the process, seven life altering books were born.

Our lives are short. Our time is valuable. We are gifted with free will. We can choose what we do with our time and our lives. It behooves us to use some of it to cultivate our minds and nurture our souls. These are the treasures that do not spoil.

The greatest gifts we have been given are talents, skills and abilities. These are obvious. What is less obvious are the gifts of time and free will. Unless we make the right choices in life, we do not advance. How or if we use our talents, skills and abilities is a choice; so is developing additional talents, skills and abilities. The quality of our life rests in our hands based on the choices we make and the actions we take.

The easiest way to advance our station in life is to increase our knowledge, but knowledge is not information. The most valuable knowledge is that which stems from experience, ours or someone else's. All of my books are based on experiential knowledge and inspiration. A little investment on your part using what I learned will yield a large return. What do I gain from making this offer?

I live to make a difference in our world. I love our incredibly beautiful planet. I want to see peace, prosperity and joint ventures the world over. My mission is to be a light that dispels darkness in all of its forms: ignorance, rigidity of heart and mind, and intolerance. I want us to have eyes that see, ears that hear and hearts that feel. By writing, teaching and by making these books available to you, I achieve my purpose.

We deserve better and it is up to us. Together, you and I can make a difference. We are all children of a loving God and we are here to do our part. We have a job ahead of us. We must accept our role and do our part.

If I, born in Syria to almost illiterate parents, in a repressive environment whose language isn't even English, am willing to do my part, so can you. We are not powerless. The more we use what we already have, the more will come our way. That is what I discovered, learned and applied in my life. If we wisely do what we now can do, more doors will open up for us. That is a promise and it is a spiritual law.

Learn, teach, serve and be an example. Let your light shine. Do not allow others to dim your light by covering it up through disempowering beliefs, fears or threats of eternal punishment. A loving God never, ever punishes His children. God only loves.

I urge you to invest in yourself. You are valuable and your contribution is needed. It is essential that we each do our part. Consider acquiring these seven books. They will not only enrich your life, but also the lives of anyone else who might happen to read them because of you.

Seven Books to Set a New Course in Life

By Shahan Shammas. Available at Amazon.com

1. A Life Altering Discovery,

not everyone has a soul

What if not everyone has a soul?

What if, of those who now have a soul, not everyone will be able to keep their soul once they die? Would you like to know how to keep yours? This book will show you, not only how to keep your soul, but also how to progressively attain conscious immortality.

Not everyone will be able to keep their soul once they die because there are more ways to lose our soul and only one way to retain it. Our soul is the one talent Christ spoke of. It is the seed dropped within us at birth as a word of God.

> Will this seed fall by the wayside where birds will devour it?
> Will it fall on hard rock where it will be scorched by heat?
> Will it fall among thorns where it will choke and suffocate?
> Or will it fall on fertile soil, establish a root system and grow to become a magnificent tree attracting the birds of the sky?

The most critical knowledge we need to have while living is how to preserve our soul so that once we die, we do not lose it. Our soul does not need to be saved from sin, for the soul never sins. It does not need to be saved from hell, suffering or eternal damnation, for the soul can never suffer. Only the physical body with its mind and emotions can suffer.

What the soul needs to be saved from is annihilation, extinction and loss forever. This will happen, according to the Parable of the Talents, if we do not invest in ourselves and cultivate our minds and hearts. We need to nurture the seed of soul and allow it to establish a root system, grow and blossom.

We are gifted with free choice. We all possess a most valuable treasure, our soul. Will we pursue trivia and squander our chance to cultivate this treasure? Or will we polish this most valuable of gems so its brilliance, brightness and light shines from the mountaintop so everyone can see it and be guided to find their way home.

This book will give us the knowledge and the resources we need to not only preserve our soul, but to cultivate it until we finally attain conscious immortality.

2. Secret Teachings of Christ, based on the parables

The secret teachings of Christ were reserved for His disciples only. Now, for the first time, they are being revealed to you. This insightful, eye-opening book will forever change how you view Christ and His parables. The Secret Teachings of Christ is a breakthrough in revealing what Christ really wanted us to know. Not only did Christ hide His most crucial teachings in the parables, He also bestowed upon us three life-altering gifts: why we should **accept and love ourselves**, why we should know that **we are important,** and that **we can make a difference**. Knowing these will surely boost our self-esteem.

The parables appear to be simple stories that Christ told His listeners. They are encoded with hidden gems of truth that He could not reveal openly lest He be stoned and killed prematurely. The parables are a clever way to preserve His teachings for posterity. The time has come to reveal these truths openly and for all. This book reveals the secret teachings of Christ based on the parables. Some of the topics include:

> What lessons can we learn from the parable of the lamp? •What does John the Baptist symbolize? •Why can't we mix new and old garments? •Who are Beelzebub and Satan? •Where is the most fertile soil to sow spiritual seeds and who is the Sower? •What exactly is the Kingdom of Heaven? Is it within us? How do we find and use it? Why is the Kingdom of Heaven like a seed, yeast, a treasure, a pearl and a net? How can discovering the Kingdom Within transform our lives? •Why did Christ have 12 disciples? •Why would a shepherd leave 99 of his sheep to seek the one he lost? •Why must we forgive? •How can we double the talents we are entrusted with? •Who is the Prodigal Son who returns home? •Did Christ come to die for our sins? Or did we kill Him because of our sins? •Why would Christ expect a barren fig tree to produce figs? •What "fertilizer" can we use to be productive ourselves? •Why does Christ refer to "wedding feasts" in His parables? Who are invited to these feasts? •What is the significance of the numbers Christ used in His parables? •Why 10 virgins? •Why is the parable of The Good Samaritan so important? •Who is our neighbor? •What does "midnight" refer to in the parables? •Is it possible to be rich and be saved? •Are Heaven and Hell real places? •What secrets lie hidden in The Lord's Last Supper? •What does the life of Jesus Christ tell us about our lives?

For a long time a veil has been placed over our eyes so we cannot see clearly. Ignorance, bias, presupposition and entrenched beliefs are components of this veil. We are responsible for our lives. If the truth is important to know, then we must do the work. We must seek, ask and knock until we have a satisfactory answer. This book will give us the knowledge we need to change course for an enlightened life.

3. Know Yourself, Love Yourself and Express Yourself

If you truly know yourself, you will love yourself and if you love yourself, you will express yourself. This perceptive, empowering book will show you how.

Is there a treasure that never spoils buried deep within us? Is this treasure a "talent" that we must develop? What exactly is this "talent"? How can we find it?

Developing this "talent" is our number one priority. It is the one thing that we must seek at the expense of all else. If we gain the whole world but do not discover what this "talent" is, we have wasted our life pursuing trivia. This "talent" is a secret hidden in plain view. Unless we know where to look, we will not see it. It is in Christianity and it is the Philosopher's Stone that the Alchemists were seeking.

Our lives would be simple had we been born with a guide for living, but we are not. We do not know why we are here, what we need to do with our lives or why we contract diseases, suffer and die. Yet, we can have meaningful answers for all of our questions. This book provides answers. It also demonstrates that we are not simply a physical body; we have astral and spiritual bodies as well. All three bodies must be cared for and nurtured so they can grow and blossom.

This book explains the purpose of life, provides a guide for intentional living and reveals many secrets such as the secret of Christianity, the secret of the Alchemists, the secrets of sleep and dreams, the secret of prayer, the secret of the mustard seed, the secret of the breath and the secret of the Millennium. Knowing these secrets will open our eyes and our hearts. We will know who we are and what we need to do with our lives. Our journey begins when we know ourselves intimately, love ourselves unconditionally and express ourselves fearlessly.

Some of the topics include:

>A Manual for Living •Does Life have a Purpose? •Why Are We Born, Live and Die? •We Are in a Theater •We Are on a Journey •We Are a Work in Progress •We Are Connected •The Nature of Our Earthly Experiences •We Are a Trinity •I AM •Knowing Our Source •The Three Names of God •How Can We Know for Certain? •Concepts of Self •Accept Yourself •Forgive Yourself •Love Yourself •Love Others •The Nature of Love •The Quest for Happiness •Be Prepared, Always •Be Fearless •Highlight Your Uniqueness •Sharpen Your Toolset •Express Yourself •Secret of Christianity •Secret of the Mustard Seed •Secret of Prayer •Secret of Sleep and Dreams •Secret of the Breath •Secret of the Alchemists •Secret of the Millennium

4. Mystery Solved! human immortality revealed

What if suddenly we understood the mysteries of life and death? Why were we born? Why do we age and die? Why do we experience pain and suffer? Why does evil exist? What if we knew that our birth was not an accident? That there is a plan for our lives and this plan is of our own choosing? What if we knew why we are attracted to specific individuals, places and situations, but not by others? What if we discovered that we have a soul and that it is of the nature of God? What if we had a better understanding of what this nature is? Would any of this make a difference? How would having answers impact our lives?

This book is based on personal experience and has the power to transform our lives for the better. The revelation I received can be yours. Peace, serenity and understanding await you. Some of the topics include:

> The Human Experience •Touching Heaven •The Spark •Reflection •Dream, The Assembly •Clues About the Nature of My Self •The Miraculous •Revelation •Disadvantages of Same Body Physical Immortality •Advantages of Cyclic Immortality •Elegance of Cyclic Immortality •What Constitutes Proof? •The Evidence •Soul, Fact or Fiction •What is Soul? •Evidence in Support of Soul •Why Do Cells Divide •Birth, Where Do We Come From? •Why Don't We Remember? •Death, Where Do We Go After We Die? •Does Life Have a Purpose? •Why Attraction? •Why Do We Experience Misery, Pain and Suffering? •Where Does Our Sense of Wonder Come From? •Why Do We Dream? •The Mystery of Identity •Understanding the Nature of Life •Making the Most of This Life •Planning for Our Next Life

The Human Experience is *unique*. Make the most of it by unravelling its mysteries. The greatest gift we have is freedom of choice. We can choose to live governed by random forces where we deal with whatever happens, or we can consciously take control of our lives. We are given "talents" and placed on a stage. We are expected to invest our talents wisely. This book will help us do just that. Act and take charge. A small investment on your part will yield a great return.

5. Listening to the Voice Within, becoming enlightened

Learning to listen to the Voice Within is the shortest route to living the abundant life. This book will show us how this practice will place us on an accelerated path to finding and living our mission in life.

There is one "gift" without which we cease to be human. Plants and animals do not have it. Only humans have it. Most do not appreciate this trademark of being human or use it effectively to advance their "Happiness Quotient." In fact, many use it to their detriment. We can discover, cultivate and learn to use this gift more effectively. It requires us to be fearless, open-minded and intent on improving our lot in life. This gift is our conscience coupled with Freedom of Choice.

Listening to The Voice Within will show us how to best use our Free Will. This book will inform, empower and liberate us. It is a guide for transformation. It will help us become enlightened beings. It will push us to grow beyond our comfort zone. To grow, we must break loose of the tethers that constrict and stifle us. Life is a journey, not a destination. If we open our minds and hearts to reason and inspiration and listen to the promptings of The Voice Within, we can be transformed. We need to discover who we are spiritually, in addition to what we are materially. Our journey of awakening starts when we let go of our fears and learn to exercise our freedom of choice. We are responsible for our lives and the decisions we make. This book is full of empowering and liberating insights that have the potential to change our lives. Here are some of the topics presented in this book:

> What is the Voice Within? ●Life as an Experiment ●How Free Am I? ●My Life as a Garden ●Obey or Disobey ●Am I My Brother's Keeper? ●Privilege ●The Transient and the Enduring ●Journey to Enough ●The Path Less Travelled ●Energy, Force, & Power ●Human Pyramid ●Natural "Enemies" of Humanity ●Memory as a Photograph ●Good, Bad and Evil ●Transformers of the World ●Perfection ●Why Attraction? Why Love? ●Insights I Live by ●Self-Examination ●Questions to Consider ●Aging, Life and Death ●Mystery of Dreams ●Raising Our Consciousness ●Soul ●Who Am I? ●The Word Made Flesh ●As Within, So Without ●In God's Image ●Living in Truth ●When Two or More Come Together ●Good News and Sad News ●Thy Kingdom Come! ●The Second Coming ●Brave, Enlightened World

Our journey of awakening starts when we let go of our fears and act with intelligence. The first decision we have to make is whether or not we are serious about improving the quality of our life by gaining knowledge and understanding. Once we are equipped with the right knowledge, we can act boldly. It will make a difference in how we see and interpret the events in our lives.

6. The Hidden Meaning & Power of the Lord's Prayer, based on the Syriac Aramaic

The Lord's Prayer is the only specific prayer Christ asked to learn and recite. Why? This book will reveal the hidden gems within the Lord's Prayer. It will also share a 12-step process to effective prayer and how to make sure our prayers are heard and answered. Additionally, this book will explain a spiritual perspective on how to establish the kingdom of heaven in our lives. Some of the topics include:

> ***Our Father who art in heaven.*** Who is this Father we are praying to? And where exactly is this heaven?
> ●***Hallowed be Thy Name.*** Do we know God's name so that we may hallow it? How can we find out what this name is? ●***Thy kingdom come.*** What exactly is this kingdom and why are we asking for it to come? Is the Kingdom of God the same as the Kingdom of Heaven? ●***Thy will be done on earth as it is in heaven.*** What does this mean? What is God's will in heaven that we want it done on earth as well? Is there any other will than that of God's will? ●***Give us this day our daily bread.*** Why are we asking only for bread? What about some meat and potatoes as well? How about some dessert while we are at it? Does this mean we do not have to earn our livelihood? ●***And lead us not into temptation.*** Who leads us into temptation? Is it God or the Devil? If it is the Devil, why are we asking God not to lead us into temptation? ●***But deliver us from evil.*** What exactly is evil? And if God does deliver us from evil, does it mean that we do not face difficulties anymore?
> ●Why did Christ teach us this specific prayer? Are there hidden gems buried within it that we need to discover?

7. A Passion for Living, a path to meaning and joy

Not much can be achieved in life without passion. Following our passion, we live a meaningful and joyous life. What can be more rewarding!

Do we know why we are here and what is the best way to live? Are we the result of an accident of nature? Were we created by God to be tested? We can have real and satisfying answers to these fundamental questions. The key is insistent desire, persistence and a demand to know. *"Ask and it will be given to you; seek and you will find; knock and the door will be opened for you."* Matt 7:7-8. This is what Christ promised us. These are active verbs. We must take the first steps. Our asking, seeking and knocking, however, must be loud, insistent and persistent until we have our answer.

To live a life of meaning and joy, we must wake up to who we are. We must live for a purpose that embodies who we want to be. We can be victimized by our circumstances or we can choose to create the life we want. This book helps us wake up, decide on something worthwhile to live for, know ourselves, decipher the meaning of life and master the art of living. We can understand why we age and die, how to release our brakes, take it easy, do what we can and enjoy ourselves. If we apply the insights in this book, we will discover our passion for living and live a life of meaning and joy. Some of the topics in this book include:

> Wakeful Living •We Do Not Have to Struggle to Succeed •We Have What It Takes •Have Something Worthwhile to Live For •Know Yourself •Decipher

the Meaning of Life and Master the Art of Living •The Blueprint of Life and Its Architect •Understand Why We Age and Die •Eight Reasons We Decide to Die •Release Your Brakes •Ignorance, Fear, Pain and Suffering •Take it Easy, Enjoy Yourself and Do What You Can •Living Like a Corporation •Willingness to Change •Dimensions of Reality

The paperback version of **A Passion for Living, a path to meaning and joy** is available only from the author. To order it for $17.00 plus $3.95 S/H. please email your request to: shahanshammas@gmail.com
Order 2 or more copies and the shipping is free. You can pay via PayPal, Venmo or Zelle.

My name and email address are:
Shahan Shammas
shahanshammas@gmail.com

Please provide you full name, mailing address and an email in case there is a question. Once I receive your payment, I will mail you the book(s).

To face the challenges of life, we need knowledge stemming from experience. If knowledge is power, these books give us the power we need to live happy, fulfilled and meaningful lives. Instead of merely passing through life, we can wake up, live with passion and make a positive difference in our lives and the lives of others. By improving the quality of our life through knowledge, the lives of those we touch will also improve. We are each valuable because we are interconnected. If J. T. through one book altered the course of my life for the better, we can do the same.

Grab this opportunity to set your life on a new course. This is your chance. Order these books and study them. You will gain understanding and valuable insight on how to master your circumstances. With understanding comes wisdom, contentment and peace of mind. You have the power, not only to improve your life, but also to impact the lives of those you care about. Often, all it takes is a small gesture such as the gift of a valuable book.

ACKNOWLEDGEMENT

I am grateful to the Cosmic for inspiration, guidance and the required resources to write this book. I appreciate the help of all those who made this book a reality especially my wife Barbara. I am indebted for her dedicated support, understanding, and patience, and for her reviewing and editing. Barbara's help and support have been invaluable. Next, I would like to thank family and friends for their continued support, especially Joe Shammas for his support and encouragement.

ABOUT THE AUTHOR

Shahan Shammas

Shahan was born in Aleppo, Syria. At the age of 15, he went to Lebanon where he entered a monastery to study and prepare to be a monk. After two years in the monastery, he left to continue his education. Shahan graduated from the American University of Beirut with a Bachelor's degree in Biology. At the age of 24, Shahan left for the United States and became a US citizen after serving three years in the Army at the medical laboratory of Fort Meade, Md. After working as an Electron Microscopist at the Walter Reed Army Medical Center for 7 years, Shahan started a new career in Information Systems. He worked for the Treasury Department until he retired. Shahan then became a teacher at the Judy Hoyer Family Learning Center where he taught Life Skills to adults for ten years. Shahan's background is in the Sciences, Religion, Philosophy and Spirituality. Shahan has lectured extensively in the areas of acquiring knowledge, raising consciousness and actualizing the human potential.

Shahan is the author of: 1. The Secret Teachings of Christ based on the parables. 2. Know Yourself, Love Yourself, Express Yourself, an inspiring guide for intentional living. 3. Mystery Solved! Human immortality revealed. 4. Listening to the Voice Within, becoming enlightened.

5. A Passion for Living, a path to meaning and joy. 6. A Life Altering Discovery! not everyone has a soul. 7. The Hidden Meaning and Power of the Lord's Prayer, based on the Syriac Aramaic.

Shahan Shammas is a cultivator of the mind. He has dedicated his life to learning and teaching. His purpose is to be a light that dispels darkness, to empower those he encounters, and to be an agent for peace.

For information about Shahan's availability for speaking engagements, workshops and seminars, please email him at: shahanshammas@gmail.com

www.ingramcontent.com/pod-product-compliance
Lightning Source LLC
Chambersburg PA
CBHW071329190426
43193CB00041B/1043